Sicilian Cuisine
recipes flavours festivals

Sicily is made of changing shapes, violent colours, intense fragrances.
The same is true of its cuisine: currants and sardines intertwine,
green and red blend, sweet and savoury embrace.
It is a triumph, an explosion, a symphony.
Cooking is an art and, in Sicily, it is sublime.

Paola Andolina

(extract from Cucina di Sicilia, Dario Flaccovio editore)

EDIZIONI AFFINITÀ ELETTIVE

Sicilian Cuisine

Flavours and recipes (from the Latin "praeceptum", meaning command, instruction, rule), but also food and wine events, food history and lots and lots of curiosities

Love for this land is the common denominator bringing together all those who contributed to the creation of this book. Many thanks to the restaurants Altamarea in Pantelleria, A Giara in Giarratana, Al Giardino di Bianca in Santa Croce Camerina, Ciacco Putia Gourmet in Marsala, Il Timone in San Vito, La Grotta in Scicli, Majore in Chiaramonte Gulfi, Osteria Il Tonno Rosso in Pozzallo, Osteria dei Sapori Perduti in Modica, Pocho in Makari (San Vito lo Capo), Ulisse in Erice. Thanks also go to the B&B Il Casolare nelle Saline in Nubia, the campsite La Pineta in San Vito lo Capo, the bakery Giummarra in Ragusa, il ritrovo Progresso di Messina, the patisseries Chiofalo in Partanna and Scimeca in Caccamo. Contributions were also made by the blogs andantecongusto, bloggerincucina, cucinachetipassa, cuochepercasa, dipastainpasta, dolcisiciliani, famedisud, fornelliprofumati, ladridiricette, martolinaincucina, palermomania, palermoviva, panzaepresenza, scattidigusto, siciliabedda, sicilia convention, siciliafan, sicilianicreativiincucina and vicaincucina. Particular thanks are due to Evelin Costa of agavepalermo for her great help and Giulia Lucchesi for her advice, support and patience. The choice of recommended wines was kindly made by Anna Ruini from Ciacco Putia Gourmet di Marsala.

Dedicated to Federica

Photographs and Illustrations:

Cover photo: top andantecongusto, shutterstock, dipastainpasta, shutterstock, sicilia convention; bottom: Riccardo Lombardo. Back cover: shutterstock.

Agavepalermo: pages 14, 21, 32, 39, 42, 46, 52, 106.
Andante con Gusto: page 24.
Atzeni Gianluca: page 51.
Aurienti Nicoletta: page 55.
Bellisiciliani: page 17.
Bianca Maria: page 71.
Ciacco Putia Gormet: page 44.
Dipastainpasta: page 58.
Famedisud: page 103.
Fornelliprofumati: page 94.
Fotolia: pages 25, 29, 35, 37, 67, 80, 81.
Ilgiornaledelcibo: page 70.
Ladridiricette: page 107.
Osteria dei Sapori Perduti: pages 43, 45, 87.
Palermomania: page 117.
Rapisarda Andrea: page 101.
Raso Nino: page 13.
Ristorante Angelino: page 60.
Rizza Elisa: page 31.
Shutterstock: pages 3, 15, 16, 19, 20, 22, 23, 26, 28, 31, 33, 35, 40, 41, 47, 48, 49, 63, 65, 69, 76, 98, 110, 111, 114, 115, 118, 119, 126, 127.
Sicilia Convention: page 113.
Vicaincucina: page 79.

GRAPHICS: Claudio Falino

TRANSLATIONS:
French: Nelly Marlier, English: Nicholas Whithorn, Russian: Dina Chashchinova, Spanish: Maria Teresa Monterisi, German: Doreen Lamek

SICILIAN CUISINE

Throughout its history Sicily has experienced the coming and going of numerous different peoples and civilisations, each of which has left behind traces on the island, as well as in its culinary traditions.

Thanks to its mild climate, the island is home to numerous spices and aromatic plants: basil, oregano, mint and rosemary. These ingredients have always been the basis for seasoning Sicilian recipes.

Phoenicians, Greeks, Carthaginians, Romans, Byzantines, Arabs, Normans, Swabians, Angevins, Aragonese, Spanish and Austrian-Bourbons pillaged and subjugated the island, but also beautified and enriched it, bringing with them the customs of their culture. We find traces of this in the ingredients and plants that the various conquerors have brought to Sicily over the centuries. The fertile soil allowed the earliest Greek settlers (8th century BC) to introduce vines. The wide variety and high quality of modern day Sicilian wines bear witness to how much production has developed. The Greeks expanded olive tree plantations and the production of oil. Olives, honey, salted or baked ricotta all bear witness to the passage of the Greek civilisation.

"...the tables were replete in both quantity and variety of foods, succulent food, delightful meals and many wrote about and took an interest in cooking". This is what Mithaecus of Syracuse, a learned and scholarly man of the 6th century BC, wrote in the first known cookery book in history: "Manual of Sicilian cuisine or of the Sicilian cook". The book extolled and taught native Greeks the art of seasoning food in the Sicilian style, which was thought to be the most refined. Families of the Greek nobility were already looking for Sicilian cooks for their households in the 5th century BC.

The mosaics in the Roman villa of Casale near Piazza Armerina depict fish and fishermen, confirming that fish was widely consumed during the Roman period (from 146 BC to 468 AD). The **Romans** introduced new methods for fishing, fish farming, the processing and conservation of fish using aromatic herbs. Moreover, since Sicily produced a lot of grain (it was the granary of Rome), the local population made and ate pasta long before Marco Polo's journey to China. Broad bean "macco", sausages and "focaccia" possibly also date from this period.

The **Byzantines** (mid-6th to 9th centuries AD) imported numerous spices, along with garlic (from Turkey), onions (from Persia), watermelons (from Turkey) and peach trees (from Persia).

Under the **Arabs** (from 827 to 1060 AD) Sicily perhaps achieved its greatest level of architectural and cultural splendour. The numerous innovations and discoveries included canalization and irrigation of fields, industrial production of sugar cane, which was the real gold rush of the age, and a refined sugar trade throughout the Mediterranean. Cane sugar was known as "*cannamele*" and "*mele*" meant honey. Significant innovations also influenced the cuisine and dishes became more varied and sophisticated. The Arabs brought with them oranges, lemons, rice (which later spread to the rest of Europe) and aubergines, imported from the Middle East (originally from China), which are elaborately depicted in paintings and carpets dating from periods earlier than 1000 AD. Rice timbales, "maiulini affucati", and "pasta 'ncaciata" are of Arab origin. Maccheroni, from the Arabic "Mu-karana and/or Makruna" (line up, place alongside), originated in Sicily, specifically in Trabia, as recounted by Al Idrisi in the "Book of Roger", describing the "tria", very thin spaghetti. Others believe that the origins of the word "maccherona" are to be found in "maccare" (to squash) from Latin or "makron" (long) from Greek. Large scale production of spaghetti, "i vermicelli", later developed in Termimi Imerese. Due to the great demand, dried pasta was introduced, easier to preserve and, thus, more suitable for export. We should not forget that pasta with sardines and

couscous in its various forms are also of Arab origin. Ricotta, sesame seeds, aniseed, saffron and cinnamon were also used by the Arabs. Refined sugar became the essential ingredient in numerous sweet dishes, such as "cassata" ("quassat" case in Arabic), marzipan and "cannoli". Snow from Etna and fruit essences were used to make "granita" and "sherbet", sorbet, the forerunner of ice-cream, invented centuries later by a Sicilian from Acitrezza, who opened the first ice-cream parlour in Paris (café Procope). Tuna fishing and tuna processing experienced considerable development under the Arabs.

The **Normans** (1060-1195) were expert hunters and brought recipes for cooking game. Other additions they made to the Sicilian menu included, salted and smoked herring, stockfish, and dried salted cod soaked in milk.

The **Swabian period** lasted from 1198 to 1266. Under the **Angevins** (1266-1282) a distinction began to be made between cuisine for the nobility, the barons who hired French cooks (known as "Monsù" in Sicilian dialect, a contracted form of "monsieur"), and simple cooking for ordinary people and inns. Later, following the French revolution, many famous cooks became unemployed and headed for other European courts. These included Naples and Palermo, which rivalled the splendour of the French court. In this way, the aristocrats could offer their guests refined French cuisine, which was very much in fashion at the time. The French also imported short crust pastry, béchamel, consommé, "gateau" ("gattò" in Sicilian) and onions instead of garlic for more delicate sauces. Other legacies of the French presence are the "Matalotta" fish soup, "Fricassé", "pastizzu" di sostanza, rustic pizza and brioches.

With the **Aragonese** (from 1282), the **Spanish** and then the **Bourbons** (up to 1860) the breaded dishes known as "empanadas" in Spain arrived, along with sponge cake, used as the base for numerous desserts and cakes. Following the discovery of America tomatoes, potatoes, peppers, prickly pears, corn and cacao all arrived. The real culinary revolution was caused by the tomato, which has become a symbol of Sicilian gastronomy. When Sicilians say "*sarsa*" they only mean tomato sauce, as if none of the other hundreds of sauces in the world existed. The wild fennel also arrived from the Canaries, brought by the Spanish. In brief, for two thousand years the gastronomic culture of Sicilian cuisine has been influenced by all the peoples that have passed through and has been handed down from one generation to the next, becoming a sign of identity for all Sicilians, both in Sicily and everywhere else in the world it has been exported.

Vincenzo Jannuzzi

LOCAL FESTIVALS IN SICILY

Festivals are exciting affairs, especially when they are events linked to local produce, the agricultural seasons and country traditions. Don't miss the chance to take part in them, there are all kinds of festivals offering plenty to eat and drink. They are growing in number every year, with the support of local councils, tourism boards and various associations. In this way typical Sicilian products are promoted: oranges, asparagus, capers, artichokes, onions, beans, prickly pears, strawberries, mushrooms, lentils, almonds, medlars, nuts, potatoes, peppers, peaches, pistachios, pears and tomatoes all have festivals dedicated to them. Oil, grapes, wine and even biblical manna and Sicilian truffles warrant festivals. Moreover, in coastal towns and villages, there are plenty of fish festivals: swordfish, stockfish, bluefish, tuna. Not forgetting cuttlefish, octopus and mussels. In the interior of the island festivals celebrate the Sicilian Black pig, wild boar, roasted pork and sausages. Other occasions are dedicated to honey, "mostarda", "cunzato" bread, "arancini", "cassatelle", "granite" and "cannoli". The best known include the **Almond Blossom Festival** in Agrigento in February/March, ChocoModica in December, the Ottobrata in Zafferana and the Couscous Fest in San Vito Lo Capo in September. In addition, there are events related to the grape harvest and the red and white wines of great character produced in Sicily. To help you, we have prepared a calendar of the various festivals, each one with a number in front of it corresponding to the one on the map of Sicily, showing where it takes place. The numbers have different colours, according to the province. Buon appetito...

JANUARY
1st week
1 **Ricotta Festival in Sant'Angelo Muxaro** (AG) - Epiphany. "A Vastasata di Nardu e Riberiu", pastoral play and Ricotta **Festival**. Tasting of local products.

FEBRUARY
1st week

2 **Bread Festival** (TP)
3 **CioccoFest (Chocolate Festival) in Partanna** (TP) - Workshops.

2nd week
4 **Sausage Festival in Chiaramonte Gulfi** (RG) – On Carnival Monday as part of the ancient costume parade.
5 **Ricotta and Local Food Festival,** Buscemi (SR)

FEBRUARY/MARCH
6 **Almond Blossom Festival in Agrigento** - Every year in the Valley of Temples, with the participation of folkloristic groups from around the world. *www.sagradelmandorlo.it*

MARCH
2nd week
7 **Cuttlefish Festival in Donnalucata** Scicli (RG) - In the old port district you can taste freshly caught cuttlefish cooked in various ways.

3rd week
8 **Tarocco Orange Festival in Francofonte** (SR) – "Le Vie del Tarocco". Tasting of local dishes based on blood oranges, entertainment, guided tours.
9 **Feast of Saint Joseph in Poggioreale, Marettimo, Salemi, Gibellina, Calatafimi** (TP). Majestic altars made of bread.

● **Easter Arches in San Biagio Platani** (AG) - Religious and contemporary bread architecture.

APRIL
● **"Cavato" Festival in Monterosso Almo** (RG) - Local homemade pasta dish served with sauce. On the occasion of the Festival of Our Lady of Sorrows.

1st week
● **Blood Orange Festival in Centuripe** (EN)

3rd week
● **Artichoke Festival in Niscemi** (CL)

4th week
● **Ricotta and Cheese Festival in Vizzini** (CT)
● **Asparagus Festival in Mirabella Imbaccari** (CT) - Spring vegetable and high quality crop.
● **Artichoke Festival in Cerda** (PA) - Traditional event.
● **"Cassatelle" Festival in Favignana** (TP) - Event dedicated to the local cake made from fried pastry filled with sweet flavoured ricotta.

MAY
● **Carrot Festival in Ispica** (RG)

1st week
● **Tomato Festival in Samperi** (RG)
● **Strawberry Festival in Cassibile** (SR) - Festival full of flavour.
● **Gastrumfest in Lentini** (SR) - Medieval cuisine.

3rd week
● **Cheese Festival in S. Stefano Quisquina** (AG)
● **Medlar Festival in Calatabiano** (CT)
● **Wild Fennel Festival in Blufi** (PA)

4th week
● **Orange Festival in Gualtieri Sicaminò** (ME)
● **Festival of Traditional Flavours in Carlentini** (SR)

last week
● **Ricotta and Cheese Festival in Poggioreale** (TP)

JUNE
1st week
● **Ricotta Festival in Mussomeli** (CL)
● **Nivarata Granita Festival in Acireale** (CT)
● **Flowering Caper Festival in Pollara** (ME) - Traditional festival on the pretty island of Salina. A host of food and wine specialities.
● **Roast Pork Festival in Sclafani Bagni** (PA) - Entertainment and historical mediaeval parade. Stands with homemade products and tasting of local dishes.

2nd week

32 **Quisquina Cheese Festival** (AG) - Festival celebrating cheese and other local produce, tasting of freshly made ricotta and other dairy and cheese products.

33 **Peppered Mussel Festival in Acicastello** (CT) - Tastings of fish based dishes.

34 **Strawberry Festival in Maletto** (CT) - Traditional and popular event on Etna.

35 **Cherry Festival in Graniti** (ME) - Display and tastings of local produce, artistic and cultural events.

36 **Cherry Festival in Chiusa Sclafani** (PA) - Tasting of local produce, guided tours.

3rd week

37 **"Vastedda cu sammuco" Festival in Troina** (EN)

4th week

38 **Anchovy Festival in Acicastello** (CT) - Concerts, local cuisine and folklore.

JULY
2nd week

39 **Swordfish Festival in Acitrezza** (CT) – On the occasion of celebrations for the local patron saint.

40 **Festival of the Turkish Heads in Scicli** (RG) - Typical local cake, during celebrations in honour of Our Lady of Milizie, patron saint of the town of Scicli.

3rd week

41 **Octopus Festival in Pozzillo** (CT) – Held in the beautiful setting of the old town of Pozzillo.

42 **Black Truffle Festival in Ferla** (SR)

43 **Stragusto** (TP) – Street food festival, tastings

4th week

44 **White Tuna Festival in Stazzo** (CT) - Event promoting the local fishing industry, including the sale and processing of fish produce.

45 **Oil Festival in Furnari** (ME) - Tasting of quality oil and local produce.

46 **Red Onion Festival in Partanna** (TP) - Two days dedicated to food, wine and art.

AUGUST
1st week

47 **Oro Rosso in Pachino** (SR) - Tomato festival.

48 **"Saperi e Sapori" in Matarocco** (TP) - Tastings, local dishes, cakes.

49 **"Busiata" Festival** (TP) - Tastings, entertainment and culinary competitions. *www.labusiata.it*

2nd week

50 **Peach and Pear Festival in Maniace** (CT) - Display and tasting of peaches and pears.

51 **Food and Wine Festival in Castiglione di Sicilia** (CT) - Traditional food and wine festival.

52 **Peach Festival in Mojo Alcantara** (ME) - Tastings of dishes made using peaches.

53 **Hazelnut Festival in Sant'Angelo di Brolo** (ME) - The old town centre hosts numerous stands displaying local products for tasting.

54 **Maccheroni Festival in Raccuia** (ME)

55 **Pasta "a Taianu" Festival in Cefalù** (PA) - This event is dedicated to a traditional dish, dating back to the Arabs, prepared to celebrate the feast day of the local patron saint "Santissimo Salvatore".

56 **"Vastedda fritta" Festival in Gratteri** (PA) - Traditional festival. Events include games, guided tours and entertainment.

57 **Fish Festival in Pozzallo** (RG) - This is one of the oldest and best known Sicilian festivals, promoting fish and other local products.

Festival of "Sapori Chiaramontani" in Chiaramonte Gulfi (RG) - Tasting of local products.
- **Onion Festival in Giarratana** (RG) - Art, traditions, taste and tastings.
- **Swordfish Festival in Avola** (SR)
- **"Calici di Stelle" in Portopalo di Capopassero** (SR) – Food and wine festival.
- **"Arancino" Festival in Rosolini** (SR) - The mediaeval town hosts the "Arancino" festival.
- **Homemade Bread Festival in Valderice** (TP) - Traditions and tastes of the past.
- **Sausage Festival in Santa Ninfa** (TP) - Tastings. Local bands and street artists.
- **Grape Festival in Alcamo** (TP) - Part of the summer season "Calici di Stelle".
- **Maccherone Festival in Calatafimi Segesta** (TP) - Food stands in the old town centre and tasting of a wide variety of pasta dishes.

3rd week
- **Cake Festival and historical parade in Sperlinga** (EN)
- **Blue Fish Festival in Capo D'Orlando** (ME) - Flavours of the sea in San Gregorio.
- **Bread Festival in Montalbano Elicona** (ME) - Event dedicated to the best cuisine of this old mediaeval town, bread and local produce.

4th week
- **"Siccagno" Tomato and Lentil Festival in Villalba** (CL) - in the Bìlici Valley. Festival dedicated to typical local products from the town.
- **Seasoned Bread Festival in Castiglione di Sicilia** (CT) - Tasting of local products.
- **Fish Festival in Giardini Naxos** (ME) - In the charming setting of the Saja marina.
- **"Ranza e Sciura" Festival in Chiusa Sclafani** (PA) - Festival dedicated to the typical Arab pizza, stuffed with onions and salted sardines.
- **Manna Festival in Pollina** (PA) - Food as sweet as honey. Tasting of local products.
- **Lentil Festival in Pellizzara** (PA) - The festival is held in the small town of Petralia Soprana. Tasting of lentils cooked according to traditional recipes.
- **Fish and Wine Festival** in Portopalo di Capo Passero (SR)
- **Homemade Bread Festival in Valderice** (TP) - Three evenings of events, games and tastings.

SEPTEMBER
1st week
- **Hazelnut Festival in Mascali** (CT)
- **Sausage Festival in Calascibetta** (EN)
- **Blue Fish Festival in Marzamemi** (SR)
- **Sudest: Wine Fest in** Siracusa - Tastings
- **"Pani Cunzato" Fest in** Scopello (TP)

1st/2nd week
- **ViniMilo Etna Wine Festival** (CT) – Promotion of wines produced around Etna.

2nd week
- **Sausage Festival in Aragona** (AG) - In honour of the town's patron Saint Vincent Ferrer.
- **Wine Festival in Montevago** (AG) – "Montevago Wine Festival" Flavours of the grape harvest.
- **Pepper Festival in Sutera** (CL) - Tastings of fried peppers with boiled potatoes and eggs.
- **"Cavatello" and Pepper Festival in Cerami** (EN) - Tastings of local peppers.
- **"Arancino" and "Sfincione" Festival in Ficarazzi** (PA) - Festival dedicated to a homemade product, prepared by local bakers following the traditional method.
- **"Cassatella" Festival in Custonaci** (TP) - Tastings of "cassatelle" in broth and fried.
- **"Sfincia" Festival in Cornino** - Custonaci (TP)

2nd/3rd/4th week
91 **Grape Harvest Festival in Piedimonte Etneo** (CT) - Tasting of food and wine products.

3rd week
92 **Etna Porcini Mushroom Festival in Fornazzo** (CT)
93 **Grain and Bread Festival in Catenanuova** (EN) - Traditional "Pisera", milling of wheat in the traditional way, with accompanying folk songs and 1940s costumes.
94 **"Arancino" Festival in Assoro** (EN)
95 **Grape Festival in Roccazzo, Chiaramonte Gulfi** (RG)
96 **"Tempu ri Capuna" in San Vito Lo Capo** (TP) - Culture, delicacies and aromas of blue fish.

3rd/4th week
97 **Couscous Fest in San Vito Lo Capo** (TP) - International Food and Wine Festival. Festival celebrating the flavour and culture of couscous as a dish of peace. *www. couscousfest.it*

4th week
98 **Fish Festival in Lipari** (ME) - Celebrations in honour of Saints Cosmas and Damian and traditional Fish Festival in Marinacorta di Lipari.
99 **Grape Harvest Festival in Pedalino** (RG) - Food and wine, folklore and culture.
100 **Wine Festival in Montevago** (AG)

4th week of September and 1st week of October
101 **Pistachio Festival in Bronte** (CT) - Bronte becomes a showroom for its famous green produce.

OCTOBER
Every Sunday
102 **"Ottobrata Zafferanese"** (CT) - Market offering typical products from Etna, stands displaying crafts and tasting of local products, in the old town centre of Zafferana Etnea.
103 **Nebrodi Black Pig and Porcini Mushroom Festival** in Cesarò (ME) - Tastings of black pig meat and porcini mushrooms from the Nebrodi mountains.

1st week
104 **Prickly Pear Festival in San Cono** (CT) - Held every October since 1984, celebrating the magnificent local fruit produced in San Cono, the "bastardone".
105 **Peach Festival in Leonforte** (EN)
106 **"Mostarda" and Prickly Pear Festival in Gagliano Castelferrato** (EN)
107 **Hazelnut Festival in Novara di Sicilia** (ME) - Festival created to promote the hazelnut harvest, part of the rich history and traditional activities of the local people and territory.
108 **Honey Festival in Sortino** (SR) - Tasting of honey and cakes and liqueurs made from this product.
109 **Red Garlic Festival in Nubia** (TP) - In the setting of the salt museum.

1st/2nd week
110 **Walnut Festival in Motta Camastra** (ME) - Entertainment, folklore and tasting of local products.

2nd week
111 **Prickly Pear Festival in Santa Margherita di Belìce** (AG) - Tastings, art, culture and folklore.

2nd/3rd week
112 **"Mostarda" Festival in Militello Val di Catania** (CT)

3rd week

13 Truffles and Autumn Flavours in Capizzi (ME) - Meetings, displays dedicated to truffles, workshops and tastings.

14 Chestnut Festival in Mezzojuso (PA) - Local products, excursions, nature, culture, art.

15 Prickly Pear Festival in Roccapalumba (PA)

16 Mushroom Fest in Castelbuono (PA) - Tastings, excursions, exhibitions, meetings and entertainment.

4th week

17 Mushroom Display and Tasting in Buccheri (SR)

18 Flavours of the Iblei in Palazzolo Acreide (SR) - Tasting of local products.

NOVEMBER

19 Pancake Festival in Ragusa

1st week

20 "Badda" Bean Festival in Polizzi Generosa (PA) - Tasting of this fine pulse, which is promoted by the international slow food movement. *www.prolocopolizzi.it*

3rd week

1 "Cassatella" (Sweet Ravioli) Festival in Agira (EN)

2 Tour of Barrels and Larders in Monforte San Giorgio (ME) - Tour discovering the folklore, food, wine and delicacies of Sicily.

3 Ethical Stockfish in Messina - Traditional Messina dish. Tastings in piazza.

4 Ferla Mushroom Fest in Caltavuturo (PA) - Weekend of tastings and guided tours, tasting genuine produce of the woods, as well as excursions and displays concerning mushrooms.

5 Autumn Festival in Sortino (SR) - Open-air tavern.

6 "Muffuletta" and Oil Festival in Poggioreale (TP) - Local products from the land of the Elymians: "infiggnulata", "vastedda" from the Belice valley, pecorino cheese.

4th week

7 Wine Festival in Nicosia (EN)

DECEMBER

1st week

8 ChocoModica (RG) - Food and wine festival dedicated to the local homemade chocolate, held in the lovely setting of the old town centre.

9 "Spincia" Days in Custonaci (TP).

2nd week

10 "Buccellato" Festival in Enna.

11 "Cuccìa" Festival in Altavilla Milicia (PA) - Tasting of "Cuccìa", a traditional dish made from wheat and mulled wine linked to veneration of Saint Lucy.

12 Wild Boar Festival in Pollina (PA) – "On the trail of wild boars" nature trails of exceptional beauty. Held in the old town centre of Centro of Pollina, tastings of local products and guided tours.

4th week

13 "Mpanata" and "Piruna" Festival in Niscemi (CL) - Festival dedicated to local baked products made using artichokes and spinach, wrapped in a special kind of puff pastry.

"Pantesca" salad

Preparation
about 30 minutes

Difficulty easy

Recommended wine
Il Bianco (Zibibbo),
Cantina Basile

Ingredients for 4 people:
- ✓ 4 medium-sized potatoes
- ✓ an onion
- ✓ 8 tomatoes
- ✓ basil
- ✓ 12 olives
- ✓ 40g of salted Pantelleria capers

- ✓ two soft salad leaves
- ✓ oil
- ✓ salt
- ✓ mackerel in oil as required

Method:

Boil the potatoes, peel and slice them.

Add the sliced tomatoes and onion, basil, olives and capers. Season with oil and a pinch of salt.

Ristorante "Altamarea", *Pantelleria*

Salted herring in orange

Preparation	Ingredients for 4 people:
about 30 minutes	✓ 2 salted smoked herrings
Difficulty easy	✓ 6 oranges, 2 of which blood oranges
Recommended wine	✓ a celery heart
Sursur,	✓ a pinch of salt
Donnafugata	✓ pepper
	✓ extra virgin olive oil

Method:

Wrap the herrings separately in sheets of tin foil; seal them shut, place onto a hot grill and cook for 5-6 minutes; then turn over and complete cooking. Take the fish out of the wrappings and remove the scales; bone the fish and recover the fillets and any eggs. Peel the oranges and cut them into medium-sized pieces, put them into a bowl and add the boned herrings and the celery heart cut into pieces. Season with plenty of oil, a little salt and freshly ground pepper. Leave to stand for a few hours before serving.

agavepalermo

Orange salad

Preparation about 10 minutes	*Ingredients for 4 people:*
Difficulty easy	✓ 4 oranges
Recommended wine	✓ 10 green or black olives
Tascante Buonora	✓ 1 sprig of parsley
(Carricante),	✓ extra virgin olive oil
Tasca d'Almerita	✓ 2 onions
	✓ salt and pepper

Method:

Peel the oranges and cut them into slices or pieces.

Place them in a salad bowl, stone the olives and add them along with the sliced onions, finely chopped parsley, oil, salt and pepper.

Mix everything well and leave it to stand for 10 minutes, then mix again and serve.

Seafood salad

Preparation	Ingredients for 4 people:	
about 60 minutes	✓ 300g of small octopuses	✓ finely chopped parsley
Difficulty difficult	✓ 150g of shrimps	✓ 1 clove of garlic
Recommended wine	✓ 200g of prawns	✓ 50 g of black olives
Haemosa	✓ 200g of cuttlefish	✓ red chilli pepper
(Chardonnay),	✓ 200g of squid	✓ extra virgin olive oil
Masseria del Feudo	✓ 300g of abalones	✓ salt
	✓ 300g of mussels	✓ lemon juice
		✓ celery leaves

Method:

Clean the octopus, squid and cuttlefish. Rinse the prawns; then, boil them all separately in salted water. Soak the mussels and abalones in salted water for a few hours, clean the mussels, getting rid of the "beard". In two separate saucepans get the mussels and abalones to open, thus: place the mussels and a tablespoon of oil in the bottom of a saucepan, put on the lid and cook on a high heat until you hear them opening (4 or 5 minutes). Peel the prawns, place them on a serving dish and add the octopus, cuttlefish and squid in pieces; add the mussels and abalones after getting rid of the valves. Season with olive oil, parsley, red chilli pepper, black olives, salt and decorate with lemon slices and celery leaves. Mix and leave to stand for about ten minutes before serving.

bellisiciliani.ru

Raw stockfish salad

Preparation about 15 minutes	*Ingredients for 4 people:* ✓ 500g of soaked, boned and sliced stockfish	✓ 1 lemon ✓ salt and pepper as required
Difficulty easy	✓ 4 ripe tomatoes	
Recommended wine Etna Bianco (Carricante), Planeta	✓ 2 spring onions ✓ oil ✓ oregano	

Method:

Rinse the fish, dry it and cut it into pieces. Wash the tomatoes and spring onions well and cut them into small pieces. Place everything onto a serving dish, season with salt, pepper, oregano and oil. Mix and eat immediately.

Prawns in lemon

Preparation	Ingredients for 4 people:
about 30 minutes	✓ 500g of prawns
Difficulty easy	✓ 25g of salted capers
Recommended wine	✓ 3 lemons
Adénzia bianco	✓ 5/6 mint leaves
(Chardonnay, Cataratto),	✓ oil
Cristo di Campobello	✓ salt and pepper as required

Method:

Peel the raw prawns and place them in a bowl.

Squeeze the lemons and pour the juice over the prawns. Season with salt and pepper.

After soaking the capers, to remove the salt, drain them well and put them in the bowl. Scent with the mint leaves and season with oil. Leave to steep, mixing occasionally.

Marinated sardines

Preparation	Ingredients for 4 people:	✓ salt and pepper
about 30 minutes	✓ 800g of sardines	
Difficulty easy	✓ 3 cloves of garlic	
Recommended wine	✓ breadcrumbs	
Baglio di Pianetto,	✓ oregano	
Insolia	✓ wine vinegar	
	✓ extra virgin olive oil	

Method:

Clean the sardines and marinate them for about 3 hours in a dish with plenty of vinegar, salt, pepper, oregano and finely chopped garlic. Keep in the fridge.

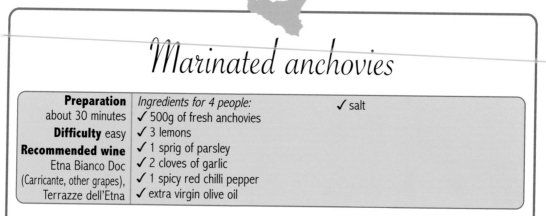

Marinated anchovies

Preparation	Ingredients for 4 people:	
about 30 minutes	✓ 500g of fresh anchovies	✓ salt
Difficulty easy	✓ 3 lemons	
Recommended wine	✓ 1 sprig of parsley	
Etna Bianco Doc	✓ 2 cloves of garlic	
(Carricante, other grapes),	✓ 1 spicy red chilli pepper	
Terrazze dell'Etna	✓ extra virgin olive oil	

Method:

Clean the anchovies, spread them open and remove the bones. Wash and dry carefully. Lay them on a deep plate, wide enough to hold them in one layer, with the interior facing upwards. Pour on the juice of two lemons, so that the anchovies are completely covered (add juice if necessary) and leave them to marinate for 24 hours, covering the dish with cling film. When the time is up, drain off the steeping liquid and place them on a serving dish. Season the fish with a little olive oil, the juice of the remaining lemon, finely chopped parsley, a few pieces of garlic and chilli pepper, a large pinch of salt and let them stand for at least an hour before serving.

Seasoned olives " Alivi cunzati "

Ingredients for 4 people:
500g of green olives, 2 cloves of garlic, basil, parsley, chilli pepper, oil and vinegar

Method:

Crush the olives and season them with finely chopped garlic, parsley, basil and chilli pepper. If you prefer to keep them in a jar, fill it with oil and a few drops of vinegar. The olives can also be seasoned with mixed pickles or with oregano and garlic covered with oil.

Olives " ammuttunate "

Ingredients for 4 people:
Large green olives, breadcrumbs, garlic, lemon, grated cheese (caciocavallo), extra virgin olive oil, parsley, anchovies, capers, salt, pepper

Method:

In a bowl mix breadcrumbs (e.g. 4 tablespoons), grated cheese (1 tablespoon), a sprinkling of finely chopped parsley, salt, pepper, a thinly chopped clove of garlic, the juice of half a lemon, oil (as much as is required to soften the mixture). Leave to stand. Cut the olives in half (lengthwise) and remove the stone. Fill with the mixture and rejoin the two halves. Place on a serving dish and decorate with available ingredients, such as anchovies, capers, onion, spring onions etc. Season with oil and lemon juice.

Evelin Costa, *agavepalermo*

Peppered mussels

Preparation	Ingredients for 4 people:	
about 45 minutes	✓ 2kg of mussels	✓ sliced homemade bread
Difficulty easy	✓ 1 glass of white wine	
Recommended wine	✓ 2 cloves of garlic	
Etna Bianco	✓ 20ml of olive oil	
(Carricante	✓ parsley	
and Chardonnay), Graci	✓ plenty of black pepper	

Method:

Carefully clean the mussels with a knife and a brush in running water to get rid of the 'beard'. Clean the garlic cloves and cut them in half. Brown the garlic with a little oil in a saucepan large enough to hold all the mussels.

Add the mussels, cook them, adding the white wine and mixing occasionally, until they are wide open. Shortly before removing from the heat add plenty of pepper and finely chopped parsley. Serve with the bread. If you wish, you can add 100g of baby/cherry tomatoes or tomato sauce to give a little more taste and colour.

Mussels au gratin

Preparation	Ingredients for 4 people:	✓ salt and pepper
about 180 minutes	✓ 1kg of mussels	
Difficulty easy	✓ 100g of breadcrumbs	
Recommended wine	✓ 50g of grated pecorino cheese	
Sole e Vento	✓ 1 sprig of parsley	
(Grillo, Zibibbo),	✓ 2 cloves of garlic	
Marco De Bartoli	✓ extra virgin olive oil	

Method:

Carefully brush and wash the mussels; then place them in a pan and get them to open by covering and heating on a high flame.

Get rid of any that remain closed and the empty half shells of the others. Place the lightly toasted breadcrumbs in a bowl, together with a little oil, finely chopped garlic and parsley, the pecorino cheese, a large pinch of salt and a sprinkling of pepper. Mix the ingredients together and spread the mixture over the remaining shells, covering the mussels. Place the mussels in a baking tin lined with tin foil, add a little oil and cook in the oven at 180° for 10 minutes.

Sicilian "Arancine"

Preparation	Ingredients for 10 arancini:	
about 60 minutes	✓ 250g of Arborio rice	✓ 100g of diced caciocavallo cheese, or alternatively mozzarella
Difficulty average	✓ 250g of Roma rice	✓ 1/2 onion
Recommended wine	✓ 1l of water	✓ 1 carrot
Per Te (Perricone),	✓ 1g of saffron pistils	✓ 1 stick of celery
Az. Agr. Fondo Antico	✓ 150g of minced veal	✓ 300g of flour
	✓ 100g of fresh peas	✓ 300g of breadcrumbs
	✓ 100ml of pureed tomato	✓ red wine
	✓ 6 eggs	✓ salt and freshly ground pepper
	✓ 100g of butter	✓ seed oil for frying

Method:

Bring the water to the boil, add salt and the rice, cover and cook on a medium heat; on completion of cooking the rice must have absorbed all the water in the saucepan. While the rice is still hot, cream it with the butter, saffron and 3 eggs and then leave it to cool. In a saucepan brown the very finely chopped celery, carrot and onion. Once the vegetables are browned, add the meat and lightly brown, adding half a glass of red wine, and finally salt, pepper and 30g of flour, being careful to avoid lumps forming. Add the pureed tomato and leave on a low heat for about an hour. In the meantime, parboil the peas for a few minutes in plenty of salted water, drain them, and cook them briefly in a frying pan with a knob of butter; once the ragù sauce is ready, finish off by adding the peas and let it cool. To prepare the "arancini", roll the rice into balls of about 5cm in diameter; make a hole in each one with your thumb and fill it with ragù sauce and a dice of caciocavallo cheese or mozzarella, then seal it again. Dip the "arancini" in the flour, then in the beaten eggs with a little salt, then in the breadcrumbs. Finally, fry them a few at a time in hot oil.

"Antica Focacceria San Francesco", *Palermo*

The history of "arancini": small Sicilian suns

The name derives from their shape and colour resembling an orange ("arancia" in Italian). In Palermo they use the feminine form "arancina", while in eastern Sicily (Catania, Siracusa, Ragusa and Messina) they prefer the masculine "arancino"; in this part of Sicily the ones made with ragù sauce may have a conical shape. Apart from the classic versions with ragù sauce or butter with mozzarella and ham, there are endless variations: with aubergines (in Catania), mushrooms, sausage, salmon, swordfish, pistachio and even with cuttlefish ink. There are also sweet versions with cacao and covered with sugar (Siracusa), chocolate (Modica) and even with nutella. The spiced rice flavoured with saffron was introduced by the Arabs, who ate it with herbs and meat. The breadcrumbs arrived later, along with tomato from America and ragù sauce from France.

"U Pani ca Meusa"

In Palermo the best known purveyor of street food is the "meusaro", who sells bread rolls "ca' meusa", also known as "vastiddaro" (from the type of bread, the name of which comes from the old French word "gastel"). The "meusaro" doesn't need to shout to draw attention to his wares because the smell of his rolls is enough to attract customers to his stall. The history of the roll "ca' meusa" is an example of how different cultures and religions can live side by side.

In the Seralcadio district of Palermo (the higher part of the modern day Capo market) there was once a large Jewish community of Spanish origins. The Jews, and previously the Saracens, introduced hygiene and dietary rules based on their religion. In the square where the "caldumai" (offal sellers) plied their trade there was also the city's abattoir, where animals were slaughtered according to religious rituals in the presence of a Rabbi or Imam. Jewish butchers were not allowed to be paid, according to their religion. Thus, they kept the offal of the animals to sell for profit. They invented a dish for Christians made from boiled offal, with ricotta or cheese, together with bread, to be eaten in the street using your hands (according to a custom introduced by the Arabs). When the Jewish community disappeared, their activity was continued by the "caciuttari", who already sold bread rolls soaked in hot lard and filled with ricotta and cheese, to which they added the offal, boiled and then fried in "saimi" (lard).

The tools of the trade for a "meusaro" are: a stove, a sloping frying pan, a skimmer, a large two-pronged fork and a carving knife for thinly slicing the boiled spleen (from a cow).

The "meusaro" is equipped with a white apron (white to begin with) and a greasy "mappina" (cloth) on which to clean his hands. The main ingredients are spleen, "scannaruzzato" (esophagus and trachea) and lungs, all boiled and then fried in lard. When you buy a roll "ca' meusa" you are asked the following question: "schietta o maritata?" (single or married?). If you are single you get a roll just with spleen, if you are married caciocavallo cheese and ricotta are added. In Palermo people would never give up eating rolls "ca' meusa", whatever the hygiene worries and despite new fashions or the introduction of modern fast food rolls or foreign products. The people of Palermo, while open to new ideas, never forget their origins, always respecting the old saying: "a panza è biddicchia / chiùssai ci nni metti / chiùssai si stinnicchia!" (the stomach is sweet, the more you fill it, the more it stretches).

Recommended wine
Il Giglio (Syrah),
Masseria del Feudo

Chick pea fritters "palermitane"

Preparation	Ingredients for 50 fritters	✓ pepper as required
about 20 minutes	✓ 500 g of chick pea flour	✓ extra virgin olive oil as required
Difficulty easy	✓ 1.5 l of water	(normally seed oil is used, but our
Recommended wine	✓ 10 g of salt	preference is for olive oil)
Miani Brut (Catarratto),	✓ 10 g of finely chopped parsley	
Castellucci Miano	✓ 10 sesame seed rolls	

Method:

Put the cold water into a large saucepan and sift the chick pea flour into it. Beat energetically with a whisk, to avoid the formation of lumps (it is important for the water to be very cold), then begin to heat on a medium flame. Add the salt and pepper and continue to mix. It is important to keep the heat medium and to keep on mixing without stopping, otherwise the mixture will all stick to the pan. When the mixture starts to thicken and boil, cook for another 10-12 minutes. Continue to mix energetically to avoid lumps forming: if any should form, get rid of them by using a hand-held food mixer. After removing from the heat, add the parsley and keep the mixture warm, covering it with cling film. Spread the mixture quickly (it must be hot) onto pizza plates (in Sicily there are special wooden utensils), to a thickness of 2-3 mm. Leave these layers to dry until they become dense, then cut them into wide medium-length strips (some pieces will be left over and can be used even though they are a different shape) and remove them from the plate without breaking them, possibly using a spatula. Heat the oil in a large frying pan and fry the fritters for a few minutes, until they are golden on both sides. Take them out of the pan using a skimming spoon and let them drain on a sheet of kitchen paper. Put into the sesame seed rolls and eat immediately.

"Pani cunzatu"

Preparation	Ingredients for 4 people:	✓ extra virgin olive oil
about 15 minutes	✓ 1 home baked durum wheat loaf	✓ white vinegar
Difficulty easy	✓ mozzarella or primosale cheese	
Recommended wine	✓ Pachino tomatoes	
Vigna di Gabri	✓ basil leaves	
(Ansonica, other	✓ capers	
grapes), Donnafugata	✓ green olives	

Method:

Cut the tomatoes and mozzarella into pieces. Finely chop the capers and basil and then place everything in a bowl, adding a little oil, a few drops of vinegar and a little garlic (optional). Spread this mixture on the bread. An alternative to mozzarella is baked ricotta (a cheese typically found in Sicily). If possible, add almond paste, finely chopped caper berries, grilled aubergines, oregano and basil.

"Sfincione palermitano"

Preparation about 100 minutes	
Difficulty average	
Recommended wine CDC Rosso, Baglio del Criso	

Ingredients for 4 people:
- ✓ 5 ripe tomatoes
- ✓ 1 onion
- ✓ grated pecorino cheese
- ✓ anchovies
- ✓ flour
- ✓ caciocavallo cheese in pieces
- ✓ oregano
- ✓ breadcrumbs
- ✓ extra virgin olive oil
- ✓ salt and pepper

Method:

Mix the flour with yeast melted in warm water and with a teaspoon of sugar. Knead the mixture until you get a very soft dough and then add salt. Put into a bowl and leave the dough to rise, covering it with a tea towel. Brown the onions in a frying pan with oil. Add the tomatoes, salt and pepper and cook for 20 minutes. Lay the dough, to a thickness of 2 cm., in a baking tin greased with oil. Place the anchovies in pieces, cover with small pieces of caciocavallo cheese, pour on the tomato sauce and sprinkle with breadcrumbs and oregano. Cook in the oven at 180° for 30 minutes.

Curiosity:

The name "sfincione" ("sfinciuni") derives from the Latin "*spongia*" (sponge) or from the Arabic "*sfang*" (fritter) in reference to the porous dough with its spongy texture. The dough, halfway between bread and pizza, is specially leavened, making it characteristically high and soft.

Breaded "Scacce"

Preparation	Ingredients for 4 perople:	For the filling
about 60 minutes	For the pasta	✓ 1 bottle of tomato puree
Difficulty average	✓ 500g of durum wheat flour	✓ basil as required
Recommended wine	✓ 200g of water	✓ salt as required
Rosso Ibleo,	✓ 20g of yeast	
Gulfi	✓ 6g of salt	

Method:

Prepare the pastry by rolling it out thinly in a round shape with a diameter of about 50cm. Add the tomato seasoned with basil, salt and grated cheese. Then add diced cheese. Roll up the pastry turning it over 2/3 times and bake in the oven in a baking tin at 250°C. After about 20 minutes, the focaccia is ready.

Panificio "Giummarra", *Ragusa*

"Scacce Modicane":
These popular snacks are available in various flavours: tomato and caciocavallo cheese, tomato and onion, ricotta, ricotta and sausage, ricotta and spinach, onion and parsley, aubergine, caciocavallo cheese and basil. All worth trying.

"Scacciata" with cauliflower

Preparation	Ingredients for 6/8 people:	
about 120 minutes	✓ 500g of dough for focaccia	✓ 2 spring onions
Difficulty average	✓ 1 medium-sized cauliflower	✓ 1 tablespoon of capers
Recommended wine	✓ 80g of anchovies pickled in oil	✓ extra virgin olive oil
Grazie Mille,	✓ 100g of black olives	✓ salt and pepper
Cantirrificio Vittoria	✓ 150g of fresh caciocavallo or tuma cheese	

Method:

Clean the cauliflower and boil the tops in plenty of salted water. Slice the onion and brown it in the frying pan with four tablespoons of oil; add the drained cauliflower and leave it to flavour for a couple of minutes. Knead the dough and roll it out in a layer about 5mm thick; then, cut out two discs, one a bit bigger than the other. Use the bigger one to cover the bottom and sides of a greased oven dish; fill with the vegetables, diced cheese, stoned and split olives, capers and small pieces of anchovy. Cover with the remaining dough and seal the edges well; brush the surface with 4 tablespoons of oil mixed with a tablespoon of water and leave to stand at room temperature for about an hour. When the time is up, bake in the oven at 220°C for about 45 minutes. When cooked, leave it to cool for a while, covered with a tea towel.

Stuffed aubergines

Preparation	Ingredients for 4 people:	
about 90 minutes	✓ 12 small aubergines	✓ 3 cloves of garlic
Difficulty easy	✓ 200g of breadcrumbs	✓ 1 cup of tomato concentrate
Recommended wine	✓ 100g of fresh provola cheese	✓ red wine
Frappato, Az. Agr. COS	✓ 40g of grated parmesan	✓ basil, parsley
	✓ 4 ripe tomatoes	✓ extra virgin olive oil, salt and pepper

Method:

Wash the aubergines, dry them and remove the tops by pulling out the stalks, make a cross cut in the area beneath and scoop out the interior with a spoon, put the interior pulp to one side, sprinkle a little salt in the cavities of the aubergines, turn them upside down and leave to stand for 10 minutes. Cut up the pulp into small pieces, place in a bowl immersed in salted water and cover. Mix together the breadcrumbs, the grated cheese, small pieces of provola, finely chopped basil, salt and pepper. Rinse out the interior of the aubergines and drain. Rinse, squeeze and brown the pulp in a frying pan with a little oil. Add the peeled chopped tomatoes to the pulp, mix, crush and cook until everything is well blended, then mix together with the breadcrumb mixture. Stuff the aubergines with this mixture, pressing it down as you gradually insert it. Brown the aubergines in oil, place them in a greased oven dish with cloves of garlic. Place on the heat and when the garlic is browned, remove it and pour on the wine. Sprinkle the lightly diluted tomato sauce over the aubergines, cover and cook for about 15 minutes.

agavepalermo

Aubergine pie

	Ingredients for 4 people:	✓ oil and salt as required
Preparation about 60 minutes	✓ 4 small aubergines	
Difficulty easy	✓ 200g of fresh sheep milk ricotta	
Recommended wine La Segreta, Planeta	✓ 200g of diced fresh cheese	
	✓ 50g of dried tomatoes pickled in oil	
	✓ 10 basil leaves	

Method:

Cut the aubergine into slices about 1/2 centimetre thick, fry in extra virgin olive oil and place on a sheet of kitchen paper. In a food mixer, blend the ricotta, basil, the drained dried tomatoes and a few slices of fried aubergine until you obtain a smooth mixture. Place an aubergine slice in a food mould about 8cm in diameter and then some of the mixture along with some cheese. Repeat these layers 4 times, finishing off with a slice of aubergine. Remove the moulds and cook in a preheated oven for about 5 minutes.

Parmigiana with baked ricotta

Preparation	Ingredients for 4 people:	
about 60 minutes	✓ 1 round purple aubergine	✓ salted ricotta
Difficulty easy	✓ 500g of tomatoes in pieces or	✓ basil
Recommended wine	pureed	✓ oil and salt
Syrah, Fondo Antico	✓ 200g of fresh cheese	✓ breadcrumbs
	✓ 1 clove of garlic	✓ egg
		✓ milk

Method:

Cut the aubergines into slices 1 cm thick. Brush these aubergine slices with oil on both sides and fry them in oil. Prepare the sauce: in a frying pan brown the garlic in oil, remove it and add the tomato, salt and pepper and cook until it congeals, add a few basil leaves. Assemble the parmigiana: alternate layers of aubergines, sauce, grated baked ricotta, fresh cheese and a few basil leaves, repeating for 3 or 4 layers and decorate with a bunch of basil. On top of the final layer pour on an egg beaten with milk and breadcrumbs to avoid it burning and to create a crust. Bake in the oven for 20 minutes.

Curiosity:

The name "parmigiana" does not refer, as many mistakenly think, to the city of Parma (it is a typical southern Italian dish) nor to the parmesan cheese, which arrived in Sicily after the Second World War (previously only local cheeses were used, in this case baked ricotta or pecorino).

It derives from "parmiciana" or "palmigiana", which in old Sicilian dialect referred to the overlapping strips of wood in shutters.

The dish took this name because of the overlapping layers of aubergines. In the past only "petronciana" type aubergines were used. This is one of many Sicilian dishes with Arab origins. It was called "al-badingia" and nowadays there are dishes very similar to the Sicilian one both in Turkish and Arab cuisine.

Sicilia 'nnamurata.altervista

Aubergine roulades

Preparation about 45 minutes	*Ingredients for 4 people:*
Difficulty easy	✓ 2 aubergines
Recommended wine Nero d'Avola, Giasira	✓ 50g of raisins
	✓ 2 tablespoons of grated pecorino cheese
	✓ 200g of stale breadcrumbs
	✓ half a cup of tomato sauce

✓ 1 sprig of parsley
✓ 1 sprig of basil
✓ extra virgin olive oil
✓ salt and pepper

Method:

Wash the aubergines, slice them and place in a colander. Sprinkle with salt and leave to stand for half an hour. In the meantime, grate the breadcrumbs and mix in a dish with the grated pecorino cheese, softened raisins, finely chopped parsley and basil, salt and a dusting of pepper. Then add the tomato sauce and blend carefully until you get a smooth mixture. Drain and dry the aubergines and fry them in plenty of hot oil. Lay them on a kitchen top and spread some of the mixture on each one.

Roll up and place the roulades in a greased baking tray. Bake in the oven for 10 minutes at 200˚. Serve hot.

Peperonata

Preparation	Ingredients for 4 people:
about 45 minutes	✓ 1kg of peppers
Difficulty easy	✓ 500g of potatoes
Recommended wine	✓ 500g of onions
Vino Bianco Bidis,	✓ 4 ripe tomatoes
Valle della Casa	✓ olive oil
	✓ salt and pepper

Method:

Slice the peppers and onions and brown in a frying pan with plenty of oil. Add the potatoes in small pieces, cover and cook on a low heat for about 20 minutes.

Sauté the tomatoes separately, then add them to the other vegetables. Leave to stand for a while, add salt and pepper as required and serve warm.

Stuffed peppers

Preparation	Ingredients for 4 people:	
about 70 minutes	✓ 4 peppers	✓ 1 clove of garlic
Difficulty average	✓ 100g of primosale cheese	✓ 1 tablespoon of pine seeds
Recommended wine	✓ 100g of breadcrumbs	✓ 1 bunch of parsley
Noto,	✓ 5dl of tomato puree	✓ 1 tablespoon of raisins
Marabino	✓ 1 bunch of basil	✓ 3 tablespoons of grated pecorino cheese
	✓ 1 onion	✓ extra virgin olive oil
	✓ 100g of diced salami	✓ salt and pepper

Method:

Slice the onion and brown it in a saucepan with 4 spoonfuls of oil; pour on the tomato puree, add salt and pepper and cook for about 10 minutes.

Wash the peppers and dry them; cut off the tops and put them to one side, remove the seeds and interior and sprinkle with salt.

Brown the breadcrumbs in a frying pan with 2 spoonfuls of oil, let them cool and add the grated pecorino cheese, salami, diced primosale cheese, pine seeds, finely chopped parsley and garlic and the previously soaked and drained raisins.

Season the mixture with a large pinch of salt, a dusting of pepper and stuff the peppers. Cover them with the tops you put aside and stand them upright in a baking tin greased with oil; pour on the tomato sauce, a dash of oil and bake in the oven at 180° for about 40 minutes.

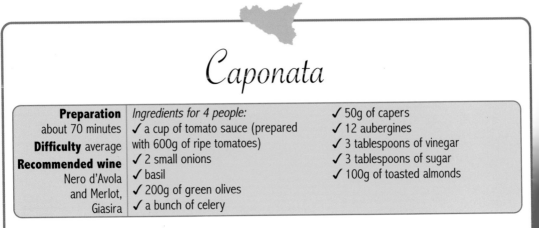

Caponata

Preparation	Ingredients for 4 people:	
about 70 minutes	✓ a cup of tomato sauce (prepared with 600g of ripe tomatoes)	✓ 50g of capers
Difficulty average		✓ 12 aubergines
Recommended wine	✓ 2 small onions	✓ 3 tablespoons of vinegar
Nero d'Avola	✓ basil	✓ 3 tablespoons of sugar
and Merlot,	✓ 200g of green olives	✓ 100g of toasted almonds
Giasira	✓ a bunch of celery	

Method:

Dice the aubergines and fry them, after leaving them for more than an hour in salted water. Separately, brown the stoned olives, capers and celery in a pan with a little oil. The celery should have been boiled previously in water for 10 minutes to soften it. Add the tomato sauce and season with the vinegar and sugar. Vinegar can be added in greater quantity than indicated, depending on personal taste. Place the aubergines in the pan as well and let them absorb the flavour of the sauce on a very low heat for a few minutes, mixing occasionally to avoid them sticking to the pan. Place the caponata on a serving dish and sprinkle with the finely chopped almonds. Serve cold, even the day after.

Ristorante "La Grotta", *Scicli*

History of "caponatina":

According to Alberto Miccichè (La Cucina, Almi editore) "caponatina" derives from caponata and he hypothesises that it comes from a typical means of expression in Sicilian dialect, in which the diminutive form is used figuratively to describe how good a food is. "Caponatina" could also be the diminutive form of caponata in the sense of a poorer dish, in that it lacks any fish ingredients and is made using only vegetables. The aubergines replace the gurnard fish.

Caciocavallo "all'Argentiera"

Preparation	Ingredients for 4 people:
about 15 minutes	✓ 400g of semi-matured caciocavallo cheese
Difficulty easy	✓ 2 cloves of garlic
Recommended wine	✓ oregano
Camporeale, Rapitalà	✓ wine vinegar
	✓ sugar

Method:

Brown the garlic in a little oil. Add the caciocavallo in slices about a centimetre thick. When it has browned on both sides, add a tablespoon of vinegar and a pinch of sugar. Let the vinegar evaporate and add the fresh oregano. Cook for a few more minutes and then serve the "caciu" hot.

History of "Caciu all'Argentera":

The name of this dish seems to originate from the story of a silversmith from the Vucciria in Palermo. He found himself in financial difficulty and could not afford to buy meat, so he prepared this dish, which gives off a smell similar to meat based dishes, in order to deceive his neighbours about his financial position.

Poached cauliflower "alla catanese"

Preparation	Ingredients for 4 people:	
about 60 minutes	✓ 2kg of "bastard" cauliflower (purple)	✓ oil as required
Difficulty average	✓ 100g of fresh pepato cheese	✓ a pinch of salt
Recommended wine	✓ 150g of salted anchovies	✓ pepper
Etna Rosso,	✓ 150g of stoned black olives	✓ 1 glass of red wine
Cusumano	✓ 10 fresh green onions	
	✓ 100g of grated pecorino cheese	

Method:

Cut the flowers of the cauliflower from the stalk, wash and slice them. Place two tablespoons of oil in the bottom of a saucepan and then cover with leaves from the cauliflower, after washing them. On top of the leaves place a layer of cauliflower slices topped with pieces of fresh pepato cheese, pieces of salted anchovy (after rinsing them in running water), stoned black olives, finely chopped green onion and grated pecorino cheese. Add salt and pepper. Make a second layer of cauliflower, topped with the same ingredients, and then another layer of cauliflower. Season with a little olive oil and pour on a glass of red wine. Insert a smaller lid into the saucepan so that it covers the cauliflower and then place a weight on the lid. Cook on a low heat for 45 minutes.

Giulia Lucchesi

Stuffed Giarratana onion

Preparation about 30 minutes	*Ingredients for 4 people:*	✓ extra virgin olive oil
Difficulty easy	✓ 4 medium sized Giarratana onions	✓ pepper
Recommended wine La Bambina, Cantine Barbera	✓ 400g of rice	
	✓ 150g of minced veal	
	✓ pureed tomato	
	✓ parsley as required	
	✓ salt	

Method:

Remove the central part of the onions, slice and brown in extra virgin olive oil. Cook the rice and prepare the tomato sauce. Add the minced meat to the onions and brown well. Add the rice, parsley, salt and pepper as required and mix everything together. Stuff the outer part of the onions with the mixture. Place in a baking tin and bake in the oven for 15 minutes. When cooked, decorate with a basil leaf. Possible variations to the stuffing include the addition of fresh diced mozzarella, diced fried aubergines and a sprinkling of salted ricotta to be put into the mixture.

Ristorante "A Giarra", *Giarratana*

Popular Palermo cuisine

In the 1700s the poorer people of Palermo did not limit themselves to listening to stories of the nobility and their chefs, they were not satisfied with smelling the tempting aroma that wafted out from their palaces, they also wanted the right to taste these delicacies. There was, however, a limit to this right and this limit was poverty. The appropriate ingredients were not available to them, no fresh fish, garden birds, quails, etc. What they could afford were vegetables, pulses, sardines (if they were not particularly fresh), fish conserved in salt or oil. They did possess, however, one very important ingredient, the most important one, imagination.

Thus, very simple foods could become perfect surrogates for the original ones and the results were delicious dishes, outright "gastronomic counterfeits".

All that was needed were sweet and sour sauces made using capers and olives, "assassunata" sauce (made with garlic and oil), breadcrumbs, raisins etc. to enhance any dish.

In this way sardines were camouflaged and turned into garden warblers (a small bird considered a delicacy), aubergines cut on the sides and fried took on the appearance of quails, aubergines also replaced the gurnard fish in "caponata", spleen was fried to give the illusion of eating "real meat", broad beans were cooked "a cunigghiu", perhaps to create the illusion that these pulses were mixed with pieces of wild rabbit, and sardines were opened up and boned to look similar to sole, considered a delicacy and known as "lenguado" by the Spanish nobility, thus Palermo sardines became "allinguate" or "sole sardines". Tuna conserved in oil was used, raisins for sweetening and pine seeds for "disinfecting" the stomach, chick peas for creating delicious fritters, offal for imitating meat stews, and nothing was thrown away, everything could be turned into delicious dishes, from the velvety leaves of the pumpkin plant, called "tenerumi", flavoured with garlic and oil, to cartilage fried in lard ("frittola") and even the leftovers from frying fritters and croquets ("arrascatura") to be eaten in a sandwich.

Evelin Costa, *agavepalermo*

Soup with "tenerumi"

Preparation	Ingredients for 4 people:	✓ olive oil
about 30 minutes	✓ 4 or 5 bunches of "tenerumi"	✓ salt and pepper
Difficulty easy	(leaves of the courgette plant)	
Recommended wine	✓ 300g of taglierine	
Sole e Vento, Az. Agr.	✓ 500g of ripe tomatoes	
Marco De Bartoli	✓ a small onion	
	✓ basil	

Method:

Clean the "tenerumi" well, choosing the softest leaves, and chop them into small pieces. Peel the tomatoes, remove the seeds and collecting the juice separately. Brown them in a frying pan with oil, the grated onion and plenty of basil. Boil the "tenerumi" in plenty of salted water and when half cooked add the pasta broken into pieces.

When the taglierine are almost cooked, reduce the water to the desired amount and add the tomatoes, onion and basil. Mix, taste for salt, pepper and oil and remove from the heat. Leave to cool in the bowls before serving.

Broad bean "macco" with wild fennel

Preparation	Ingredients for 4 people:	
about 120 minutes	✓ 250g of dried shelled broad beans	✓ extra virgin olive oil
Difficulty easy	two bunches of "qualeddro"	✓ salt as required
Recommended wine	(Mediterranean cabbage)	✓ pepper grains
Grillo Parlante,	✓ a bunch of wild fennel	
Az. Agr. Fondo Antico	✓ two small leeks	
	✓ 100g of fresh breadcrumbs	

Method:

Soak the broad beans for half a day. Drain and rinse them. In a saucepan brown the leeks in extra virgin olive oil, pepper grains and water. Cook until the leeks are browned. Add the broad beans and cover the contents with water. Wash the wild fennel, finely chop it and add to the rest. Cook for about 2 hours adding water if necessary. In the meantime clean the "qualeddro" getting rid of the harder stalks and cook it in plenty of lightly salted water. Once it is ready, drain and keep to one side. Toast the breadcrumbs in a frying pan. The broad beans are ready when they are no longer hard when you bite them. Leave to cool and blend everything using a handheld blender, until it is almost pureed. Taste for salt. Serve in a dish with the "qualeddro", toasted breadcrumbs and fresh oil on top. Decorate the dish with a sprig of wild fennel.

"Ciacco Putia Gourmet", *Marsala*

Osteria dei Sapori Perduti

Pasta "Tagghiarini" with broad beans

Preparation	*Ingredients for 4 people:*
about 120 minutes	✓ dried shelled broad beans
Difficulty easy	✓ fresh wild fennel
Recommended wine	✓ 400g of fresh tagliolini
Nero d'Avola, Curma,	✓ onion
Az. Agr. Armosa	✓ tomato puree
	✓ salt and extra virgin olive oil

Method:

Boil the broad beans. Skim them and then season with finely chopped onion, fresh wild fennel in pieces, salt and pureed tomato to add colour to the dish.

Cook everything for about an hour.

When the broad beans become creamy, add a little water and bring to the boil; add the fresh tagliolini. Serve this creamy dish with a little extra virgin olive oil.

"Osteria dei Sapori Perduti", *Modica*

Pasta and beans "Pasta ca triaca"

Preparation	Ingredients for 6 people:	✓ 1 carrot
about 90 minutes	✓ 1kg of fresh borlotti beans shelled	✓ salt and pepper as required
Difficulty easy	just before cooking	
Recommended wine	✓ 200g of ditali or maltagliati type	
Cerasuolo di Vittoria,	pasta	
Valle dell'Acate	✓ 1 stick of celery	
	✓ 1 onion	

Method:

Place in a saucepan, preferably earthenware, the beans, thinly sliced onion, tomato, chopped carrot and chopped celery.

Cover and simmer on a low heat for 90 minutes in two litres of cold water. In this way the skin of the beans will not wrinkle. Before adding the pasta, taste for salt, then add the ditali and cook. Finally, add extra virgin olive oil, pepper and serve the pasta and beans hot.

agavepalermo

Baked Anelletti

Preparation	Ingredients for 4 people:	
about 90 minutes	✓ 300g of anelletti	✓ 100g of mozzarella
Difficulty average	✓ 150g of minced veal	✓ 100ml of red wine
Recommended wine	✓ 150g of minced pork	✓ 1 green onion
Due Dei (Grillo Metodo	✓ 150g of peas	✓ 5 tablespoons of olive oil
Classico),	✓ 200g of pureed tomato	✓ butter, breadcrumbs
Roberto Trancida	✓ 100g of caciocavallo cheese	✓ salt and pepper as required

Method:

Brown the finely chopped green onion in olive oil and then add the mince, browning it. Add the wine and, when it has evaporated, the pureed tomato, salt and pepper. Cook this sauce on a low heat for 20 minutes. Be careful not to let the sauce dry out, adding hot water if necessary.

Add the peas and cook a little while longer. Boil the anelletti separately in salted water, draining them when half cooked. Mix them with the ragù sauce, grated caciocavallo cheese and diced mozzarella. Grease an oven dish with butter, sprinkle on the breadcrumbs, tip in the pasta and cover with more grated cheese. Bake in a pre-heated oven for 40 minutes at 180°. Leave in the oven for 10 minutes after turning off and then serve.

Curiosity:

This baked pasta dish is very popular in Palermo and is generally reserved for holidays because, although it is quick to prepare, the slow cooking of the ragù sauce takes at least 2 hours.

Spaghetti "alla norma"

Preparation	Ingredients for 4 people:	
about 60 minutes	✓ 350g of spaghetti	✓ 2 aubergines
Difficulty easy	✓ 400g of pureed tomato	✓ 80g of hard salted ricotta
Recommended wine	✓ 1 yellow onion	✓ 2 tablespoons of olive oil
Il Cratere Rosso,	✓ 1/2 teaspoon of sugar	
Terrazza dell'Etna	✓ 4 basil leaves	
	✓ salt as required	

Method:

Brown the onion in a pan, add the pureed tomato, salt, sugar and basil and cook for at least an hour. The sliced or diced aubergines must be softened in water or coarse salt for 30 minutes to remove the bitter taste and then fried in hot oil.

Drain them using kitchen paper. In the meantime, boil the pasta in a saucepan with plenty of salted water, add the aubergines to the tomato sauce and when the pasta is ready and drained, mix it briefly in the pan with the sauce.

Serve with plenty of grated baked ricotta.

History of pasta "alla norma":

In 1831 Vincenzo Bellini, one of the most famous 19th century opera composers (la Sonnambula, i Puritani, la Norma), who was from Catania, composed the opera Norma in just three months, after which it opened at the Scala in Milan. The aria Casta Diva immediately made this opera famous to the extent that the expression "sembra la Norma" ("pari 'a Norma" in Catania dialect) became a synonym for beautiful well made things, worthy of admiration. Later, in 1920, during a lunch at which the guests included the actors Angelo Musco

and Turi Pandolfini, as well as the poet and playwright Nino Martoglio, the hostess and cook served this new spaghetti dish and it was greatly appreciated.

After a few mouthfuls Martoglio complimented the cook: "signura Saridda chista è 'na vera Norma" (signora Saridda this is a genuine Norma).

The name stuck and this pasta dish from Catania has since become one of the most popular and best known Sicilian recipes in the world.

Pasta with broccoli "arriminati"

Preparation	Ingredients for 4 people:	✓ an onion
about 60 minutes	✓ 350g of maccheroni	✓ a tablespoon of tomato conserve
Difficulty average	✓ 50g of sultanas (softened in water	✓ a glass of olive oil
Recommended wine	for 15 minutes)	✓ two fistfuls of grated pecorino
Grillo,	✓ 5g of pine seeds	cheese
Azienda Agricola	✓ one small cauliflower	✓ 3 salted anchovies
Nino Barraco	✓ 4 basil leaves	✓ salt

Method:

The name "arriminato" (mixed) derives from the action of continually mixing, which helps to make the cauliflower creamy. In Palermo cauliflowers are known as broccoli.

Boil the cauliflower in plenty of salted water. Drain when it is al dente. Put some oil in a saucepan and brown the onion. Add the tomato conserve diluted in a glass of hot water. Cover and cook on a medium heat. Now add the cauliflower. Place the washed and boned anchovies in a pan with the remaining oil and dissolve them on a low heat, pressing on them with a fork. Now add the anchovies to the cauliflower, with the sultanas (drained and dried) and the pine seeds. Mix everything together and leave to stand. Cook the pasta in plenty of salted water, drain when it is al dente, place in a tureen and add the cauliflower, sauce and the grated pecorino cheese mixed with the finely chopped basil. Mix well and serve.

siciliani creativi in cucina –foto Gianluca Atzeni

Pasta with broccoli

Preparation about 60 minutes	*Ingredients for 4 people:* ✓ 400g of maccheroni	✓ 1 onion ✓ 5 basil leaves
Difficulty easy	✓ 600g of broccoli	✓ 1 tablespoon of tomato conserve
Recommended wine Deliella (Nero d'Avola), Feudi Principi di Butera	✓ 70g of grated pecorino ✓ 50g of raisins ✓ 50g of pine seeds ✓ 3 salted anchovy fillets	✓ extra virgin olive oil ✓ salt

Method:

Boil the broccoli in plenty of salted water and drain them when they are al dente. Brown the sliced onion in a frying pan with a little oil and add the tomato conserve diluted in a glass of hot water. Cover and cook on a very low heat for about 10 minutes, then add the broccoli in pieces. Melt the anchovy fillets in a frying pan with a little oil, crushing them with a fork. Add the anchovies to the broccoli, then the raisins, previously softened in warm water and dried, and the pine seeds. Mix and leave to stand for 5 more minutes.

Cook the pasta in plenty of salted water and mix in a soup bowl with the broccoli and sauce, the grated pecorino cheese and the finely chopped basil. Serve hot.

Spaghetti with fried courgettes

Preparation about 45 minutes	*Ingredients for 4 people:*
Difficulty easy	✓ 400g of spaghetti
Recommended wine Bianco di Nera, Azienda Agricola Milazzo	✓ 2 green courgettes suitable for frying
	✓ 1 glass of extra virgin olive oil
	✓ grated salted ricotta or pecorino cheese
	✓ a clove of garlic
	✓ fresh mint
	✓ salt and pepper as required

Method:

Wash the courgettes, trim the ends and then slice them and sprinkle with salt. Crush the garlic and brown it in a frying pan with oil, remove the garlic and fry the courgettes. Drain them and keep them hot on a plate, putting the frying oil to one side.

Boil the pasta in salted water, drain it when it is al dente and season it with the oil used to fry the courgettes. Sprinkle with black pepper, add the courgettes, sprinkle with the cheese and add a few fresh mint leaves.

agavepalermo

Pasta "Incaciata"

Preparation about 90 minutes	*Ingredients for 4 people:*
Difficulty average	✓ 400g of maccheroni
Recommended wine Faro, Azienda La Fauci	✓ 1kg of ripe tomatoes ✓ 150g of fresh caciocavallo cheese ✓ 150g of minced meat ✓ 50g of mortadella ✓ 100g of grated pecorino cheese

✓ 2 hard boiled eggs
✓ 4 aubergines
✓ 2 cloves of garlic
✓ 1/2 glass of dry white wine
✓ 2/3 basil leaves
✓ extra virgin olive oil
✓ salt and pepper

Method:

This is the Messina version of the classic Sicilian baked pasta. Brown the garlic cloves in a little oil, then add the tomatoes, previously parboiled, peeled, seeds removed and cut into pieces. Add salt, if needed, and then the basil when cooking is finished. In the meantime, slice the aubergines, let the bitter liquid drain from them and then fry. In a saucepan brown the minced meat in plenty of oil, add the wine and let it evaporate and complete cooking adding a few tablespoons of the tomato sauce you prepared. Cook the pasta in plenty of salted water, drain it when it is al dente and season it in a tureen with the tomato sauce. In an oven dish alternate layers of pasta with layers of meat, fried aubergines, grated cheese, boiled egg slices, caciocavallo cheese and mortadella in pieces, finely chopped basil. Complete the final layer with aubergines, tomato sauce and plenty of grated pecorino cheese. Bake in the oven at a medium temperature for about 20 minutes.

"'ncasciata" and "'ncaciata":

This is a baked pasta dish (originally made with pork and cauliflower), "'ncasciata" deriving from "incassata" (packed), placed in a casserole dish, not to be confused with pasta "'ncaciata", with lots of cacio cheese, a typical dish from the province of Messina.

Rice timbale

	Ingredients for 4 people:	
Preparation about 90 minutes	✓ 500g of rice	✓ 2 eggs
Difficulty average	✓ 100g of tomato concentrate	✓ 1/2 onion
Recommended wine Rosso di Verzella (Nerello Mascalese, Nerello Cappuccio)	✓ 200g of minced pork	✓ 50g of breadcrumbs
	✓ 50g of mortadella	✓ 1 bunch of parsley
	✓ 100g of primosale cheese	✓ extra virgin olive oil, salt and pepper
	✓ 50g of grated pecorino cheese	
	✓ 2 aubergines	

Method:

Mix the mince with the dampened breadcrumbs, an egg, the finely chopped parsley and the grat-

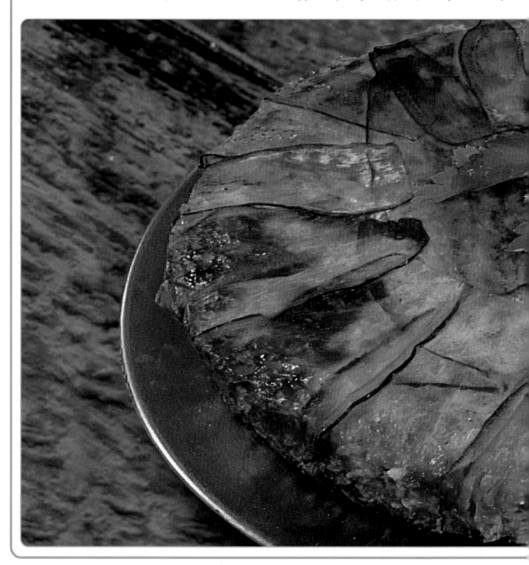

ed pecorino cheese. Brown the mixture in a frying pan on a high flame for a few minutes and mix it with the tomato concentrate sauce prepared with sliced onion and oil. Dilute with water and complete cooking of the meat.

Cook the rice in plenty of salted water, drain when it is al dente and season in a soup tureen with some of the ragù sauce. While the rice is cooling, fry the sliced aubergines in plenty of oil, after having drained the bitter liquid, and hard boil the remaining egg. In a greased baking tin sprinkled with breadcrumbs prepare alternate layers of rice and fried aubergines, sliced boiled egg, slices of primosale cheese, mortadella and ragù sauce.

Finish off the final layer with rice dampened with a little oil and sprinkled with breadcrumbs. Bake in the oven for about an hour at a medium temperature and serve warm.

Nicoletta Aurienti - cuochepercasa

Busiate with green pesto

Preparation about 35 minutes	*Ingredients for 4 people:*
Difficulty easy	✓ 400g of busiate
Recommended wine Anthilia, Donnafugata	✓ 4 cloves of garlic
	✓ 100g of basil
	✓ 100g of parsley
	✓ 100g of celery sticks
	✓ 100g of white almonds
	✓ 200g of Mazara prawns
	✓ 100g of tuna eggs
	✓ oil, salt and pepper as required

Method:

Take the basil, parsley, celery, almonds, garlic and finely chop them all with a little oil.

Place the mixture in a saucepan, add the prawns and cook for 2-3 minutes, adding salt and making sure the flavours mix.

Bring plenty of salted water to the boil and cook the busiate; drain them when they are al dente, then place them in a bowl with the pesto, mix well and sprinkle with the grated tuna eggs.

Camping "La Pineta", *San Vito Lo Capo*

Ricotta ravioli in pork sauce

	Ingredients for 4 people:	✓ nutmeg as required
Preparation about 150 minutes	*For the pasta*	✓ salt as required
Difficulty average	✓ 200g of durum wheat flour	*For the pork sauce*
Recommended wine Syrah 2014, Azienda Agicola. Foderà	✓ 3 eggs	✓ 300g of pork bacon
	✓ salt as required	✓ 150g of tomato concentrate
	For the filling	✓ 50g of onion
	✓ 500g of ricotta	✓ 5g of black pepper
	✓ 50g of salted caciocavallo cheese	✓ 20g of salt
	✓ 1 egg yolk	✓ water as required

Method:

Knead the ingredients for the pasta, lay it out and place the filling on the pastry, giving it the shape you prefer. Brown the onion, fry the bacon, add the tomato concentrate, salt, black pepper and water to dilute the sauce.

Cook the sauce for at least 2 hours on a low heat. Serve with a little basil as decoration.

Ristorante "Al Giardino di Bianca", *Santa Croce Camerina*

Pasta with sardines

Preparation about 60 minutes	*Ingredients for 4 people:*
Difficulty average	✓ 320g of spaghetti or maccheroncini
Recommended wine Marsala Sup. Ris. 10 anni, Curatolo Arini	✓ 300g of fresh sardines
	✓ 300g of wild fennel
	✓ 100g of breadcrumbs
	✓ 40g of raisins
	✓ 40g of pine seeds

✓ 4 salted anchovies or sardines
✓ 1 sachet of saffron
✓ 1 clove of garlic
✓ extra virgin olive oil
✓ salt and pepper

Method:

Clean the fennel, remove the hardest part, wash and boil in salted water (in a saucepan with a colander) drain and chop into small pieces. Put to one side the water used for boiling, which will be used again for boiling the pasta. Place the raisins to soak in warm water. In a frying pan brown the anchovies with the garlic, then remove the garlic and add the boned sardines, after removing the heads and tails, cut into large pieces or whole if small. Add the pine seeds, the drained and squeezed raisins, the wild fennel, the saffron dissolved in a little of the water used for boiling, salt and pepper and cook for 5 minutes. In the meantime, boil the pasta using the same water in which the fennel was cooked, drain, mix with the sauce in the frying pan, adding a few spoonfuls of hot water and serve with a sprinkling of toasted breadcrumbs.

dipastaimpasta

Pasta with sardines... "a mare" (at sea)

Sicilians make great use of irony, also towards themselves, joking about their own straitened financial circumstances. This dish was so simple that its ingredients didn't even include cheap sardines, which stayed out ... "a mare" (at sea).

Spaghetti in tuna sauce "alla trapanese"

	Ingredients for 4 people:	
Preparation about 60 minutes	✓ 400g of spaghetti	✓ dry white wine
Difficulty easy	✓ 300g of fresh tuna	✓ extra virgin olive oil
Recommended wine	✓ 4 ripe tomatoes	✓ salt
Viognier,	✓ 1 tablespoon of salted capers	✓ pepper
Barone Montalta	✓ 1 clove of garlic	✓ 50g of shelled toasted almonds (optional)
	✓ 1 sprig of mint	

Method:

Soak the tuna in water and salt for an hour; then drain, dry and dice it, after removing the skin. Brown the garlic in a saucepan with 5 tablespoons of oil, add the fish and brown it, mixing it in the seasoning. Add the wine and wait until it evaporates; then, remove the garlic and add the peeled tomatoes, having removed the seeds and sliced them, and the desalted capers. Pour in a ladleful of hot water; sprinkle with crushed mint and continue to cook for about 20 minutes. Cook the pasta in plenty of salted water; drain when it is al dente and mix it with the sauce in the saucepan. If desired, sprinkle with the finely chopped toasted almonds before serving.

Ristorante "Angelino", *Trapani*

Busiate "al pesto trapanese"

Preparation	Ingredients for 4 people:	
about 35 minutes	✓ 1kg of fresh red tomatoes	✓ 400g of fresh pasta (Busiate)
Difficulty easy	✓ 100g of toasted almonds	✓ 100g of breadcrumbs for decoration
Recommended wine	✓ 4 cloves of "nubia" red garlic	
Sherazade,	✓ a small bunch of basil	
Cantina Donnafugata	✓ olive oil as required	
	✓ salt, pepper	

Method:

Rinse the tomatoes and place them in hot water for 5 minutes; then, peel them and chop them into large pieces. Crush the almonds for a while in a mortar, with a little salt, then place in a dish and use the mortar to crush the garlic, basil and a little salt until you get a smooth mixture. Add the tomato and continue to crush with the pestle so that the ingredients blend well. Then put the pesto into the dish with the almonds, olive oil, salt and a little pepper; mix and leave to stand for half an hour. Cook the busiate; season them with the pesto and decorate with toasted breadcrumbs, prepared thus: place the breadcrumbs in a frying pan with olive oil and a little chilli pepper, mix and cook on a low heat until it becomes toasted.

Ristorante Pizzeria "Ulisse", *Erice*

Spaghetti with mussels

Preparation	Ingredients for 6 people:
about 60 minutes	✓ 2kg of whole mussels
Difficulty easy	✓ 600g of spaghetti
Recommended wine	✓ 2 cloves of garlic
Ciuri,	✓ a bunch of parsley
Cantina	✓ olive oil
Terrazze dell'Etna	✓ salt and pepper

Method:

Heat the mussels in a covered frying pan on a low heat until they all open. Remove from the shells and filter the water left in the pan. In a saucepan brown the finely chopped garlic in plenty of oil. Add the filtered water from the mussels, season with pepper and leave to thicken for a few minutes. Add the mussels to the saucepan and leave them to flavour in the sauce for five minutes. Turn off the heat and sprinkle with plenty of finely chopped parsley. Cook the pasta al dente and mix with the mussels in a soup dish.

Spaghetti with sea urchins

Preparation	Ingredients for 6 people:	
about 60 minutes	✓ 600g of spaghetti	✓ olive oil
Difficulty easy	✓ 60 sea urchins (50 if the gonads are	✓ salt
Recommended wine	very full of eggs)	
Ammàno (Cataratto),	✓ 2 cloves of garlic	
Cantine Barbera	✓ ground white pepper	
	✓ a bunch of parsley	

Method:

Split open the sea urchins with a pair of scissors and carefully collect their eggs in a bowl. Lightly brown the chopped garlic in plenty of oil.
Remove the frying pan from the heat, and let the oil cool. Boil the spaghetti, drain when it is al dente and season it in a soup dish with the oil used for browning, plenty of pepper, the sea urchin eggs and a fistful of finely chopped parsley.

Spaghetti with cuttlefish ink

Preparation	Ingredients for 4 people:	✓ 2 tablespoons of Sicilian tomato extract or a good concentrate
about 80 minutes	✓ 400g of spaghetti	✓ 750g of tomato sauce
Difficulty average	✓ 1 large or two small cuttlefish (with ink sac)	✓ extra virgin olive oil
Recommended wine Creation, Cantina Giasira	✓ 2 medium-sized onions	✓ salt and pepper
	✓ 1 glass of dry white wine	

Method:

Clean the cuttlefish keeping the ink sac intact. For the sauce you only need to use the head and tentacles, which should be chopped into very small pieces. Heat 3 tablespoons of oil in a large frying pan and add the tentacles. Add the onion almost immediately then a glass of dry white wine and let it evaporate. Add the tomato extract diluted in a little water. Add the tomato sauce, heat it for a few moments, then add the ink sac. With the help of a wooden spoon, break the sac; the sauce will begin to get darker until it becomes completely black. Boil the spaghetti until it is al dente, place it in the frying pan with the sauce and finish cooking, adding a little cooking water from time to time if necessary. Place on plates and serve.

Spaghetti "co niuru de sicci"
A cook in Catania has invented "u ripiddu nivicatu" (the snow-topped mountain), rice with cuttlefish ink in a pyramid shape "snow-topped" with ricotta and spicy tomato sauce. It represents Etna, "a muntagna" dark and black, snow-topped and in eruption.

Spaghetti with clams

Preparation	Ingredients for 4 people:	✓ salt and pepper
about 45 minutes	✓ 500g of clams	
Difficulty easy	✓ 400g of spaghetti	
Recommended wine SurSur (Grillo), Donnafugata	✓ 2 cloves of garlic	
	✓ extra virgin olive oil	
	✓ parsley	

Method:

Clean the clams well, place in a covered frying pan and heat until they all open. Remove from the heat and filter the liquid left in the pan into a bowl. Heat the oil in a frying pan with a clove of garlic, which should be removed as soon as it browns. Add the open clams, the finely chopped parsley, salt and pepper. Cook for a few minutes, add the liquid you previously conserved and cook for 5 more minutes. Cook the spaghetti, drain and tip into the frying pan with the clams. Cook for 2 minutes, add a little fresh parsley and freshly ground black pepper just before serving.

Spaghetti with swordfish and roe

	Ingredients for 4 people:
Preparation about 45 minutes	✓ 200g of swordfish
Difficulty easy	✓ 80g of tuna roe
Recommended wine Lighea, Donnafugata	✓ Pachino cherry tomatoes
	✓ 400g of spaghetti
	✓ olive oil and garlic as required

Method:

The name derives from "batarickh", an ancient Arab method of fishing. The roe is the pressed, salted and seasoned sac of tuna or swordfish eggs.

Brown the garlic, add the roughly chopped swordfish, fry lightly and add a little cooking water. When the spaghetti is al dente, drain, place in the pan and mix with the tuna roe.

If desired, chilli pepper and parsley can be added. Garnish the dish grated roe and the cherry tomatoes and serve.

Ristorante "Il Timone", *San Vito Lo Capo*

Spaghetti with roe

Preparation	Ingredients for 6 people:	✓ parsley
about 30 minutes	✓ 600g of spaghetti	✓ salt
Difficulty easy	✓ 120g of roe (tuna eggs)	
Recommended wine	✓ half a chilli pepper	
Cuvée Brut	✓ olive oil	
(Chardonnay), Tenute	✓ garlic	
delle Terre Nere	✓ basil	

Method:

Finely chop garlic and parsley and brown them in a saucepan with a little oil. Add the chilli pepper in pieces and the roe sliced and softened in oil.

Continually mix with a wooden spoon. Boil the spaghetti in salted water until it is al dente, drain and mix with the hot sauce.

Sprinkle the fresh basil leaves on top. Serve without adding any kind of cheese.

Fish couscous with essences

Preparation about 180 minutes	*Ingredients for 4 people:*
Difficulty difficult	✓ 1kg of semolina
Recommended wine Grappoli del Grillo, Az. Agr. De Bartoli	✓ 2 onions
	✓ 1 head of garlic
	✓ 1kg of mixed fish for broth and as much as you want for frying
	✓ 2l of tomato (concentrated or pureed)
	✓ 150g of almonds
	✓ lemon, chilli pepper
	✓ cinnamon, laurel and parsley
	✓ oil, salt and pepper as required

Method:

Tip the semolina into the "mafaradda" (terracotta dish) bit by bit and use your right hand in a circular motion to split it into very small clumps while sprinkling it with a little water with your left hand. Season the semolina in the dish with oil, salt, pepper, cinnamon and finely chopped onion and parsley, then place it in the couscous pan with a few laurel leaves and lemon rinds between each layer. Steam for about an hour, adding to the boiling water a bunch of herbs, cloves and a few small fish for broth. In the meantime prepare the fish soup: brown the sliced onions in plenty of oil. Add the tomato, salt and pepper, a pinch of chilli pepper, cinnamon and plenty of pesto made from garlic cloves, parsley and almonds. Cook for 20 minutes and towards the end add the fish for broth, which you had previously cleaned. Tip the steamed couscous into a large soup tureen together with half of the soup and some of the fish pieces. Cover with a woollen cloth and leave to stand for 45 minutes. Serve with the rest of the fish soup. As desired, add on top mixed fried fish, fried in olive oil. Various types of couscous can be made, replacing the fish with pork, lamb, pulses and vegetables and using different herbs and flavours, according to personal taste.

Albergo Ristorante "Pocho", Makar

Anchovies "alla catanese" ("masculini")

Preparation	Ingredients for 4 people:	
about 60 minutes	✓ 1kg of fresh anchovies	✓ 50g of desalted capers
Difficulty average	✓ 40g of stoned green olives	✓ pecorino cheese
Recommended wine	✓ 30g of pine seeds	✓ garlic and parsley
Cuvée Brut,	✓ 2 tablespoons of breadcrumbs	✓ juice of one orange
Cantina Terrazze	✓ half a lemon	✓ extra virgin olive oil
dell'Etna	✓ half a glass of dry white wine	✓ salt and pepper

Method:

Clean the anchovies, removing the head, bones and interiors; then, wash them in running water and dry them with kitchen paper.

Chop up the green olives and pine seeds. Grease an oven dish with oil and put in the anchovies, place some lemon slices, the chopped olives and pine seeds and a previously prepared mixture of breadcrumbs, capers, pecorino cheese, garlic and parsley, on top. Add a large pinch of salt, a sprinkling of pepper and a dash of oil.

Sprinkle on the wine and complete by repeating the layers in the same order. Finish off with a dusting of breadcrumbs. Place the dish in a pre-heated oven at 200° and cook for 15 minutes, dampening with filtered orange juice at the halfway point. When cooked, remove from the oven and serve immediately.

ilgiornaledelcibo

Sicilian sardine patties

Preparation about 45 minutes	Ingredients for 4 people:
Difficulty easy	✓ 600g of fresh sardines weighed when already cleaned and opened
Recommended wine Etna Bianco Nerina, Girolamo Russo	✓ two eggs ✓ currants and pine seeds ✓ 150g of breadcrumbs ✓ 50g of grated parmesan ✓ two cloves of garlic ✓ parsley as required

✓ salt and pepper
✓ extra virgin olive oil
✓ 700g bottle of tomato puree
✓ small onion
✓ salt and sugar (for the sauce)
✓ fistful of boiled wild fennel
✓ pasta (bronze drawn rigatoni)

Method:

Remove the heads, bones and interiors of the sardines, open them up and wash in running water. Add salt and leave them to drain in a colander.

Cut them into small pieces and add the eggs, breadcrumbs, parmesan, currants and pine seeds, pepper, and finely chopped garlic and parsley. Dampen your hands, roll up the mixture into patties, fry them in oil and drain on kitchen paper. Brown a finely chopped onion in a large frying pan, add the tomato puree, a little sugar and salt. When it comes to the boil, add the sardine patties and a fistful of pre-boiled wild fennel. Cook until the sauce thickens. If you decide to use it as a sauce for pasta, place a saucepan of water on the heat and when it boils, add the rigatoni and cook until it is al dente. Season the pasta with the sauce and the sardine patties.

Maria Bianca, *blog panzaepresenza*

Sardines "allinguate"

Preparation about 45 minutes	*Ingredients for 6 people:*
Difficulty easy	✓ 1kg of sardines
Recommended wine Settecento, Azienda Agricola Cusumano	✓ a glass of white vinegar
	✓ reground durum wheat flour
	✓ extra virgin olive oil

Method:

Clean the sardines, removing the interior and heads, scale them, open up, remove the bones leaving the tail attached. Wash them in running water. Place in a bowl and completely cover with the vinegar, cover with cling film and keep in the fridge for about an hour. When the time is up, drain the sardines well, cover in flour and fry in very hot oil until they turn golden brown on both sides. Drain on a sheet of kitchen paper. Add salt and serve hot.

Maria Floriti, *Palermo Viva*

Curiosity:

During the Spanish domination of Sicily, the poorer classes used to copy some of the fashionable dishes of the nobility using cheaper ingredients. Thus, sardines were used instead of the sole that the Spanish nobility called "lenguado". This is the origin of the name sardines "a lenguado" (sole sardines) or sardines "allinguate" in Sicilian. Soaking the fish in vinegar was also a way of avoiding health risks, as it was not always very fresh.

Sardines "a beccafico"

Preparation	Ingredients for 6 people:	✓ 3 tablespoons of sugar
about 60 minutes	✓ 1.5kg of fresh sardines	✓ 1 bunch of parsley
Difficulty average	✓ 7 salted anchovies	✓ 1 bunch of basil
Recommended wine	✓ 100g of raisins	✓ 1sprig of laurel
Birra Marinette,	✓ 100g of pine seeds	✓ extra virgin olive oil
Cantirrificio Vittoria	✓ 2 lemons	✓ salt and pepper
	✓ 200g of breadcrumbs	

Method:

Clean and bone the sardines, open them up, wash and dry them carefully. Desalt, bone and chop finely, then mix them with the breadcrumbs, previously browned in oil, the raisins, soaked in warm water and drained, the pine seeds and a few tablespoons of finely chopped parsley. Carefully mix together all the ingredients and then add salt and pepper. Lay the mixture on the open sardines and close them up using a cocktail stick. Place the sardines in a lightly greased baking tin, alternating them with laurel leaves. Prepare a sauce dissolving the sugar in the juice of a lemon, adding a few spoonfuls of oil. Cover the sardines with the sauce and then bake them in the oven at 200°C for about 20 minutes. Before serving sprinkle with finely chopped basil and decorate with slices of lemon.

Sardines "a Beccafico"
The name of this popular recipe, not to be found on the tables of the nobility, derives from "beccafico" (garden warbler), a chubby bird, just like the sardines with their stuffing. A tasty dish to be eaten cold.

Stockfish "agghiotta"

Preparation about 45 minutes	*Ingredients for 4 people:*	✓ 15/20 green olives in brine, well rinsed, stoned and cut in two
Difficulty average	✓ 1kg of soaked stockfish	
Recommended wine Case Bianche, Azienda Enza La Fauci	✓ 1/1.2kg of potatoes	✓ 0.75l of tomato puree or as much as required to cover the fish (diluted with a glass of water)
	✓ 1 fistful of desalted and washed capers	
	✓ 1 heart of celery	✓ extra virgin olive oil
	✓ 1 large onion	

Method:

Use plenty of oil to grease a light saucepan (preferably an old fashioned aluminium one, otherwise a "modern" one will do), and insert the thinly sliced onion, the olives, the celery cut into pieces, the capers and fry on a medium heat without browning the onion. Add the tomato puree diluted with water, salt and pepper. Bring this to the boil and then add the stockfish, cut into pieces. Cook for about 15 minutes. N.B.: the stockfish "ghiotta" should not be mixed using spoons or ladles, just shake the saucepan, otherwise it will fall apart! Add the peeled potatoes cut into large pieces, add salt and cook on a low heat for about 40-45 minutes or until the potatoes are cooked, adding a ladle of hot water if necessary to stop the sauce drying out, and shaking the saucepan from time to time. "Ghiotta" is a unique dish but if you use plenty of tomato puree, the sauce left over is an excellent accompaniment for a plate of pasta.

The difference between "baccalà" and "stoccafisso"
It is important to clarify the difference between "baccalà" and "stoccafisso" (stockfish). In both cases it is cod but stockfish is dried in the sun and open air while baccalà is pressed in salt in barrels. Stockfish is used in the traditional Messina "ghiotta" recipe.

Stuffed squid

Preparation	Ingredients for 4 people:	✓ 1/2 glass of dry white wine
about 60 minutes	✓ 1kg of squid	✓ extra virgin olive oil
Difficulty average	✓ 2 dry-salted anchovies	✓ red chilli pepper powder
Recommended wine	✓ 50g of green olives	✓ salt
Nozze d'Oro	✓ 30g of dry-salted capers	
(Chardonnay),	✓ 2 cloves of garlic	
Tasca d'Almerita	✓ breadcrumbs	

Method:

Clean, wash and dry the squid. Finely chop and mix the olives, one clove of garlic, the desalted anchovies and capers washed in salted water. Then mix these with the breadcrumbs, a tablespoon of water and enough oil to make the mixture soft and spongy. Stuff the squids with the mixture obtained and close them up with cooking string or a wooden skewer. Brown the crushed garlic in an earthenware pan with a little oil and season with a pinch of chilli pepper. Remove the garlic and place the squid in the pan. Once they have used up all their own water, add the wine. When the wine has evaporated as well, add salt and a ladle of hot water, which should suffice until the squid is completely cooked, in other words, when it has softened well. It is also possible to add pieces of fresh pecorino cheese to the stuffing if you want an even tastier version.

Swordfish "agghiotta"

Preparation	Ingredients for 4 people:	
about 60 minutes	✓ 4 slices of swordfish	extra virgin olive oil
Difficulty average	✓ 1 clove of garlic	salt
Recommended wine	✓ 250g of peeled tomatoes	
Shiarà (Cataratto),	✓ 150g of stoned green olives	
Castellucci Miano	✓ 1 bunch of parsley	
	✓ 1 stick of celery	

Method:

Finely chop the onion and lightly brown it in a saucepan with 1/2 glass of oil and finely chopped garlic, celery and parsley. Add the crushed tomatoes, capers, sliced olives, a large pinch of salt, a sprinkling of pepper and cook on a medium heat for about 10 minutes; then pour on 1/2 cup of hot water and bring to the boil. Wash and skin the fish, dry it and place in the saucepan. Cover with a few tablespoons of sauce and cook on a low heat for 20 minutes.

"agghiotta"

This name is given to dishes favoured by greedy people. Dishes that stimulate your taste buds, whet your appetite and make your mouth water.

Swordfish roulades

Preparation about 45 minutes	*Ingredients for 4 people:*
Difficulty average	✓ 500g of swordfish in slices of which
Recommended wine Coste al Vento (Grillo), Cantine Barbera	✓ 50g browned and finely chopped
	✓ 70g of grated caciocavallo cheese
	✓ 150g of breadcrumbs
	✓ 30g of capers
	✓ 50g of green olives

✓ 1 sprig of parsley
✓ 50g of olive oil
✓ 50g of tomato sauce
✓ an onion, laurel leaves, salt and pepper

Method:

For the filling: in a bowl mix the breadcrumbs, cheese, browned and finely chopped swordfish, capers, stoned olives and finely chopped parsley; add salt and pepper to flavour.

Knead everything with the tomato sauce and olive oil.

The filling should be smooth and soft. Open up the swordfish slices as much as possible, lay on the mixture and roll them up. Place the roulades on a skewer alternating laurel leaves and pieces of raw onion. Grill or bake in the oven for about 15 minutes.

Swordfish "alla palermitana"

Preparation about 20 minutes	*Ingredients for 4 people:*
Difficulty easy	✓ 4 slices of swordfish
Recommended wine Grillo Parlante, Cantina Fondo Antico	✓ grated caciocavallo cheese
	✓ breadcrumbs
	✓ extra virgin olive oil
	✓ 1 clove of garlic
	✓ 7/8 mint leaves
	✓ parsley as required
	✓ salt and pepper

Method:

Marinade the swordfish in oil, garlic and mint for about 15 minutes.
Drain and cover with the breadcrumbs to which you have added the grated caciocavallo cheese, salt, pepper and finely chopped parsley. Cook on a very hot hotplate for about 3/4 minutes on each side. Serve hot.

www.vicaincucina.com

Swordfish "al salmoriglio"

Preparation about 30 minutes	*Ingredients for 4 people:*
Difficulty easy	✓ 4 slices of swordfish
Recommended wine Grillo, GVA Canicatti	✓ 1/2 glass of extra virgin olive oil
	✓ 2 lemons
	✓ salt

Method:

Pour the oil into a bowl; add the lemon juice, a large pinch of salt, a pinch of oregano, a dusting of pepper, and beat with a fork until you get a smooth sauce.

Sprinkle the slices of fish with salt and grill them on a hot plate; transfer them to a serving dish, pour on the "salmoriglio" sauce and serve.

Tuna "alla marinara"

	Ingredients for 4 people:	✓ a few basil leaves
Preparation about 90 minutes	✓ 4 slices of fresh tuna 1.5cm thick	✓ oregano, salt and pepper
Difficulty easy	✓ 400g of tomatoes	
Recommended wine Naisi, Nero d'Avola, Brugnano	✓ 100g of stoned black olives	
	✓ 2 tablespoons of desalted capers	
	✓ 1 clove of garlic	
	✓ 6 tablespoons of extra virgin olive oil	

Method:

Finely chop the herbs and garlic and add oil, salt and pepper in a dish together with the tuna and leave to marinate for 1 hour in the fridge.

Heat the oven and slice the tomatoes. Place the slices of tuna in an oven dish together with the marinade, the tomatoes, capers and olives. Add a dash of oil and cook in the oven for 15 minutes. Serve directly from the oven dish.

Baked tuna

Preparation	Ingredients for 4 people:
about 160 minutes	✓ 4 slices of fresh tuna
Difficulty easy	✓ 1 onion
Recommended wine	✓ 1 lemon
Mille e una Notte (Nero	✓ 1 bunch of parsley
d'Avola and other	✓ extra virgin olive oil
grapes), Donnafugata	✓ salt and pepper

Method:

Finely chop the onion and parsley, place in a mixing bowl and blend them together with the filtered juice of a lemon and a couple of glasses of olive oil. Place the slices of tuna in the marinade and leave for about 2 hours. Then place the tuna and the sauce in an oven dish and bake at a medium temperature for about 40 minutes.

Grilled tuna

Preparation	Ingredients for 4 people:	
about 30 minutes	✓ 1 red tuna slice weighing about 1.2kg making sure it is fresh (better if previously frozen) bought from a trustworthy fishmonger	✓ 1 bunch of chopped herbs (mint, thyme, marjoram, rosemary)
Difficulty easy		✓ 1 finely chopped clove of garlic
Recommended wine		✓ 1 tablespoon of red wine vinegar
Sole dei Padri (Syrah), Principi di Spadafora	✓ 3 Pachino "costoluto" tomatoes cut into segments	✓ 25g of coarse salt
	✓ 1 cucumber (sliced in a "half moon" shape)	✓ 1/2 glass of fruity extra virgin olive oil
	✓ 1 Tropea red onion (thinly sliced)	✓ 3 turns of a black pepper mill
	✓ 50g of desalted Sicilian capers	✓ balsamic vinegar reduction as required

Method:

Cut the tuna into four large steaks, about 300g each. Marinate lightly for about 15 minutes with the chopped herbs, the clove of garlic, warm extra virgin olive oil, coarse salt and vinegar. Lay the tomatoes, cucumber and onion alternately on a plate.

Heat the grill to a medium-high temperature. Grill the tuna steaks for about 40 seconds each side. Place the tuna on the plate adding a few spoonfuls of marinade on the tuna and the vegetables. Decorate with a few drops of balsamic vinegar reduction.

Osteria "Il Tonno Rosso", *Pozzallo*

Tuna with garlic

Preparation about 70 minutes	Ingredients for 4 people: ✓ salt
Difficulty easy	✓ 4 slices of tuna
Recommended wine Grillo, Alessandro di Camporeale	✓ 1 laurel leaf ✓ 3 cloves of garlic ✓ 1 bunch of parsley ✓ vinegar ✓ extra virgin olive oil

Method:

Place the tuna in cold salted water for an hour; then rinse it, dry it with kitchen paper and fry it in a frying pan with the laurel and plenty of hot oil.

Then drain the fish slices and place them on a serving dish. Brown the crushed garlic in a frying pan with oil; pour on 1/2 glass of vinegar and let it evaporate.

Sprinkle with the finely chopped parsley and pour the seasoning evenly over the fish. Serve after a few hours.

Grouper with cherry tomatoes and olives

Preparation	Ingredients for 2 people:	
about 30 minutes	✓ 2 slices of grouper with skin	✓ pepper
Difficulty easy	✓ 100g of Pachino cherry tomatoes	✓ extra virgin olive oil
Recommended wine	✓ 50g of stoned black olives	
Leone,	✓ 1 clove of garlic	
Azienda Tasca	✓ oregano	
d'Almerita	✓ salt	

Method:

Carefully slice the fish. Heat the oil in a non-stick frying pan, then add the garlic, the cherry tomatoes cut in half and the olives.

Insert the fish with the skin facing down, add salt and pepper and flavour with oregano. Cover and cook on a low heat for a few minutes, turning the fish just once to avoid it falling apart. Serve with plenty of seasoning.

Federica Gelso Giulian

Fish soup

Preparation about 60 minutes	*Ingredients for 4 people:*
Difficulty average	✓ 1.5l of fish broth (made with the leftovers of the scorpion fish)
Recommended wine Cerasuolo di Vittoria Docg (Frappato e Nero d'Avola), Gulfi	✓ 2 tablespoons of finely chopped tomato
	✓ 1 teaspoon of finely chopped parsley
	✓ 4 scorpion fish fillets (400g ca.) already boned and cut into small cubes

✓ 2 tablespoons of extra virgin olive oil
✓ 150g of fresh fettuccine cut into small pieces
✓ 1 pinch of dry ground chilli pepper
✓ salt and pepper as required

Method:

Bring the broth to the boil, add the tomato, fettuccine, scorpion fish, parsley, basil, chilli pepper, salt and pepper.

Continue to simmer until the pasta is cooked, add oil and serve hot.

Ristorante "Filippino", *Lipari*

"Agglassato" ("Aggrassatu")

Preparation	Ingredients for 4 people:	
about 90 minutes	✓ 1kg of veal, beef or shoulder	✓ 2 leaves of laurel
Difficulty average	✓ 1kg of potatoes	✓ 4 leaves of sage
Recommended wine	✓ 1kg of white onions	✓ 200g of extra virgin olive oil
Cygnus (Nero d'Avola e	✓ 1 small tomato	✓ 1/2 glass of white wine
Cabernet) Tasca d'Almerita	✓ 1 sprig of rosemary	✓ salt and pepper as required

Method:

Cut the meat into medium-sized pieces. Cut the onions into thin slices, lightly brown them in plenty of oil then continue cooking on a low heat with hot water and mix. Add the meat to the onion, add the wine and then the crushed skinned tomato. Add salt, pepper and herbs, cover the meat with hot water, cover and cook on a low heat for 60 minutes, until the meat completely softens and the sauce acquires the right consistency.

While cooking, check the bottom of the saucepan and add hot water if necessary. If you want potatoes, dice them and fry for 5 minutes, browning rather than cooking them, before adding them to the onion glaze and the meat. Cook everything together for about 10 minutes, carefully mixing. The "aggrassato" sauce is an excellent accompaniment for pasta.

Giulia Lucches

Curiosity:

"Aggrassato" is a very old Sicilian recipe, the best known of Palermo's traditional meat dishes, a dish for Sundays and holidays. It consists of slow-cooked beef, veal or chicken with lots of onion. There are an infinite number of variations with vegetables, particularly with potatoes, cooked in different ways in each town, village or household. The quantity of the glaze obtained depends on the quantity of onions.

Ostería del Saporí Perduti

Rabbit "alla stimpirata"

Preparation	Ingredients for 4 people:	
about 45 minutes	✓ rabbit pieces	✓ baked black olives
Difficulty average	✓ celery	✓ half a stock cube
Recommended wine	✓ onion	✓ rosemary and sage
Nero d'Avola,	✓ carrot	
Passo delle Mule,	✓ garlic	
Duca di Salaparuta	✓ white wine	

Method:

First of all place the pieces of rabbit in a bowl with water and vinegar for about 20 minutes. You can use any part of the rabbit.

Remove it, rinse and dry well. In a frying pan place oil, a whole garlic, a few shredded leaves of sage and rosemary, the celery, carrot and onion, all finely chopped.

Brown for a minute or so and then add the meat. Cook well and then add a glass of white wine and let it evaporate.

Meat and potato stew

Preparation about 60 minutes	*Ingredients for 4 people:*	✓ extra virgin olive oil
Difficulty easy	✓ 700g of lean beef pieces	✓ salt and pepper as required
Recommended wine Perricone, Tenute Orestiadi	✓ 1 onion	
	✓ 1kg of potatoes	
	✓ 1 tablespoon of tomato extract	
	✓ 1 sprig of parsley	
	✓ half a glass of dry white wine	

Method:

Thinly slice the onion and brown it in a saucepan with four tablespoons of oil. Add the beef pieces and brown them on a medium heat.

Add the white wine and let it evaporate. Add the tomato extract dissolved in a cup of hot water. Cover with water, add salt and pepper and cook for 30 minutes.

Add the potatoes after peeling them and cutting them into pieces and finish cooking, adding water as required.

Lamb with potatoes

	Ingredients for 4 people:	✓ extra virgin olive oil
Preparation about 90 minutes	✓ 1.5 kg of lamb	✓ grated cheese
Difficulty average	✓ 2 cloves of garlic	
Recommended wine Nero d'Avola, Chiaramonte	✓ 1kg of potatoes	
	✓ parsley as required	
	✓ salt as required	
	✓ red pepper as required	

Method:

Cut the lamb into pieces, wash and dry it well. Peel the potatoes and cut them into not too small slices; prepare the rosemary, parsley, clean the garlic and cut it into small slices.

Place the lamb in a large baking tin and season with oil, salt and red pepper.

Season the potatoes with oil, salt, parsley, red pepper and mix well; place the pieces of lamb on top of the potatoes with some rosemary and a slice of garlic under each piece; sprinkle some cheese on the lamb and cook in the oven at 180°. After 20 minutes, turn the lamb over.

Ristorante "A Giarra", *Giarratana*

"Falsomagro" - "Braciolone"

Preparation	Ingredients for 4 people:	
about 90 minutes	✓ a 500g round slice of meat about	✓ 50g of raisins and pine seeds
Difficulty average	20cm in diameter	✓ 20g of breadcrumbs
Recommended wine	✓ 2 hard boiled eggs	✓ half an onion
Tancredi,	✓ 100g of fresh caciocavallo cheese	✓ 100g of lard
Donnafugata	✓ 50g of salami	✓ 200g of tomato extract
	✓ 50g of grated caciocavallo cheese	✓ half a glass of red wine

Method:

Lay the slice of meat out on a marble worktop and lightly beat it, paying attention not to break it. Grease it with a little lard and tip on the breadcrumbs mixed with the grated caciocavallo cheese, raisins and pine seeds, the sliced hard boiled eggs, salami and pieces of fresh cheese.

Add salt and pepper. Roll the meat up, making sure that the filling stays inside. Tie up with string, first lengthwise and then across the middle, pulling the string tight, and giving it a uniform shape. Brown on a high flame in the lard, then remove the meat and use the same pan to brown the onion and dissolve the tomato extract, adding a little warm water until it becomes creamy. Add the wine and let it evaporate, replace the meat in the pan, half cover it with water and cook on a low heat for about 90 minutes.

When cooked, remove the meat from the pan and leave it to cool completely before slicing it, not too thinly. Lay the slices on a serving dish without heating to avoid spoiling them. Pour on the very hot sauce before serving.

"Braciolone" - "Falsomagro" - "Farsumauru":
The name of this typical Sicilian recipe comes from the translation or adaptation of the French word "farce", in Sicilian "far-su" (mistakenly translated into Italian as "falso" or false) and from the Sicilian adjective "mauro" (in Italian "magro" or thin).

Roasted pork shank

Preparation	Ingredients for 4 people:	
about 270 minutes	✓ 4 pork shanks	✓ sage
Difficulty average	✓ 1l of vegetable broth	✓ rosemary
Recommended wine	✓ plenty of red wine	
La Segreta Rosso,	✓ 2 cloves of garlic	
Planeta	✓ thyme	
	✓ laurel	

Method:

Place the pork shanks in a large container with the wine, garlic, and bunch of herbs and leave to marinate for at least 3 hours. After the 3 hours are up, remove the shanks and brown them in oil. Place the shanks in an oven dish lined with oven paper and put in the oven, adding the wine and herbs from the marinade.

Cover with tin foil and cook in the oven at 200° for an hour, adding the vegetable broth if necessary to avoid it drying out. Remove the tin foil and continue cooking for 30 minutes. Once cooking is completed serve the shanks with the filtered cooking liquid and accompanied by potatoes.

Stuffed pork chop

Preparation	Ingredients for 4 people:
about 90 minutes	✓ 4 thick pork chops
Difficulty average	✓ 4 portions of minced pork loin
Recommended wine	✓ 4 cubes of ragusano cheese
Cerasuolo di Vittoria	✓ 4 cubes of hard-boiled egg
(Frappato and Nero	✓ 4 cubes of salami
d'Avola), Az. Agr. COS	✓ lard, onion and salt as required

Method:

Make an opening in the chops and fill with minced loin, the ragusano cheese, boiled egg and salami in the quantities indicated. Close up the opening.

Melt the lard in a frying pan, then place the chops in the pan and brown, add the sliced onion and complete the browning, add some broth and let it evaporate, then cook on a medium heat for about 50 minutes, adding some water if necessary. Serve hot.

Ristorante "Majore", *Chiaramonte Gulfi*

Escalopes with Marsala

Preparation	Ingredients for 4 people:
about 20 minutes	✓ 6 slices of veal
Difficulty easy	✓ 1/2 glass of Marsala
Recommended wine	✓ 70g of butter
Marsala SOM,	✓ flour
Mirabella	✓ salt and pepper as required

Method:

Melt 50g of butter in a frying pan, place the slices of meat in the pan and brown them on a high flame, one minute each side.

Season with salt and pepper, then add the Marsala and two teaspoons of water. Continue cooking until the wine has almost completely evaporated and a thick sauce has formed.

Put the meat on a hot plate.

To the pan add 20g of butter mixed with flour and melt the butter until there is a thick sauce to pour over the meat.

fornelli profumati

Breaded roast veal "alla palermitana"

Preparation about 30 minutes	*Ingredients for 4 people:*
Difficulty easy	✓ 4 slices of lean veal for roasting
Recommended wine Altavilla della Corte, Firriato	✓ 30g of lard
	✓ 150g of breadcrumbs
	✓ 1 laurel leaf
	✓ salt and pepper

Method:

Dry the slices of meat with kitchen paper, cover them on one side with plenty of lard and place them on the breadcrumbs seasoned with finely chopped laurel, salt and pepper, then cover the other side with lard as well and place it on the breadcrumbs. Grill on a medium heat so that the lard melts slowly and gives flavour to the meat.

Veal roulades "alla messinese"

Preparation	Ingredients for 6 people:
about 45 minutes	✓ 800g of veal for roulades
Difficulty average	✓ 200g of fresh cheese
Recommended wine	✓ 100g of breadcrumbs
Obli,	✓ 50g of grated parmesan
Azienda Enza La Fauci	✓ a sprig of parsley
	✓ extra virgin olive oil

Method:

Lay out the thin slices of meat on a marble top, season with a pinch of salt and dampen them with oil. Mix the breadcrumbs with the parmesan, finely chopped parsley and diced cheese. Place a tablespoon of this mixture on each slice of meat, roll up the meat to make small roulades. Attach them onto the skewers, dip in oil and breadcrumbs and grill, paying attention not to over-cook them.

scatti di gusto

Meatballs in sauce

Preparation about 45 minutes	*Ingredients for 4 people:*
Difficulty easy	✓ 500g of minced meat
Recommended wine Sachia (Perricone), Caruso and Minnini	✓ 1kg of tomatoes
	✓ 80g of grated pecorino cheese
	✓ 100g of mortadella or 50g of sausage
	✓ 1 egg

✓ 1 onion
✓ 1/2 glass of milk
✓ finely chopped basil
✓ finely chopped parsley
✓ oil, salt and pepper

Method:

Prepare the sauce with the sliced tomatoes, onion, basil and salt. Cook for 30 minutes and then puree. In the meantime, mix the minced meat with the mortadella or sausage, the breadcrumbs, the grated cheese, the egg, salt and pepper in a bowl; season with the parsley and basil.
Knead and, if necessary, add a little milk to keep the mixture soft.
Make meatballs to be fried in a frying pan in hot oil. Place the meatballs in the sauce and cook for 10 minutes.

History of the "granita":

The "granita" has its roots in the Arab domination, when sugar cane was first grown in Sicily to cater for the Arabs' custom of preparing infusions using water, sugar, fruit, herbs and spices. in mediaeval Sicily there was an profession known as "nivarolo", who gathered snow from mountains or plateaus in winter and kept in "neviere" underground or in caves, and then transported it down using mules or carts. The snow was grated and used to make "sherbet" sorbets and ice-cream by adding fruit syrups, flowers or lemon juice. The oldest known sorbet seems to be the one made with jasmine ("scurzunera"). This recipe was known as "rattata". In the 12th century snow mixed with sea salt was used for refrigeration, by means of the endothermic process, the sorbets being frozen by placing them in containers surrounded by ice and salt. Thus was born the sump, a wooden vat containing a zinc bucket, which was turned using a crank. The hollow interspace was filled with salt and snow in a sack. The contents of the sump were frozen by removing heat. Impalpable to the palate, the "granita" made in this way, using water, sugar and fruit, replaced the "rattata". In the 20th century the sump was replaced by the ice-cream maker, making it possible to produce the unmistakable creamy mixture, airless and full of flavour, that has become the Sicilian "granita".

Lemon granita

Ingredients for 6 people:
glasses of 100% lemon juice, 180g of sugar

Method:

Bring the sugar to the boil with 4 glasses of water and cook for 5 minutes. Wait until the syrup obtained cools down, then add the lemon juice. Place in the freezer in a metal container and turn it over once every 20-30 minutes while it freezes. The granita will be ready after about 3-4 hours.

Pasticceria "Chiofalo", *Partanna*

Preparation
about 45 minutes
Difficulty easy

Almond granita

Ingredients for 4 people: 150g of shelled almonds, 20g of shelled bitter almonds, 150g of sugar

Method:

Bring to the boil 1l of water and leave it to cool. Parboil the almonds for a few moments separately, peel them and crush them in a mortar with the sugar until you get a fine powder, then put them through a sieve. Add this mixture to the boiled water, place in the freezer for a couple of hours, stirring from time to time, until you obtain a soft sorbet.

Coffee granita

Ingredients for 4 people: 1l of water, 300g of sugar, 300g of ground coffee, 1/2 tablespoon of vanilla, 1l of whipped cream, coffee beans for decoration

Method:

Make the coffee in a coffee pot and pour it into a container together with the sugar, vanilla and water. If you have an ice-cream maker, pour the mixture in and let it stir slowly until it becomes almost creamy (not too liquid, not too thick). If you don't have an ice-cream maker, place it in the freezer for a couple of hours. Be careful not to let the granita become too hard, whisking it from time to time until it turns creamy. Half fill the glasses and then top them up with the whipped cream. Decorate with a few coffee beans and serve with the indispensable brioche.

Bar "Progresso", *Messina*

Black mulberry granita

Ingredients for 4 people: 400g of mulberries, 200g of sugar, 750ml of water, the juice of one lemon

Method:

Carefully wash the mulberries, then put them through a sieve or, better still, whisk them. Add the lemon juice and mix. Heat the water with the sugar, stirring until it comes to the boil. The sugar must dissolve completely and, at this point, leave the syrup to cool. Join the two mixtures together and stir carefully, place in a container (steel or glass) in the freezer and wait for it to solidify. The mixture should be stirred from time to time; after about 5/6 hours your mixture should be frozen; whisk it again and you will get a kind of sorbet with a light creamy consistency. Your mulberry granita is now ready; serve with a warm brioche.

Lemon sorbet

Ingredients for 4 people:
130g of lemon juice, 250ml of water, 170g of granulated sugar, 30ml of limoncello, 30g of egg whites

Method:

To prepare lemon sorbet pour the egg whites into a bowl and whisk. When it has become partially whipped, as can be seen from the froth on the surface, sprinkle on 30 grams of sugar, while continuing to whisk.

The mixture is ready when it becomes white and frothy and can be put to one side.

Squeeze the lemons, from which you will get about 130g of juice, filter the mixture through a colander to make sure there is no pulp residue and pour the juice into a bowl already containing the water.

With the help of a whisk, lightly beat, adding the remaining 140 grams of sugar and adding the egg whites a little at a time so as not to deflate the soft mixture too much.

When everything is well mixed, add the limoncello and mix again. Pour the mixture into an ice-cream maker (follow the instructions for your ice-cream maker to see how to proceed) and switch on. When the lemon sorbet has taken on the classic creamy consistency you can put it into glasses and serve.

Peach sorbet

Ingredients for 6 people:
4dl of water, 400g of sugar, 1kg of white peaches, juice of 2 lemons

Method:

Pour the water into a saucepan with the sugar and place on a low heat, stirring from time to time. When the sugar has dissolved turn up the heat and bring to the boil, continuing for 3 minutes. Remove from the heat, leave the syrup to cool and cover it. Peel the ripe peaches, remove the stone, slice them and cut into small pieces.

Pass through a sieve, mix with the lemon juice and the syrup. Leave to cool and then pour the mixture into an ice-cream maker.

Orange sorbet

Ingredients for 4 people:
220g of sugar, 6 large oranges, 250ml of mineral water, a few mint leaves

Method:

Grate the rind of an orange, place in a saucepan with the sugar and water and boil lightly for 20 minutes. Leave the syrup to cool, filter and keep the rind to one side.

Pour the syrup into a bowl with the juice obtained from squeezing the oranges. Mix and place in the freezer for about 1 hour until the mixture begins to harden.

Mix every half hour or so with a fork to keep it soft and, half an hour before serving, add the rind and put back in the freezer for another 30-40 minutes.

Serve in dessert cups and decorate with a few mint leaves.

extract from "Fame di sud"

Cinnamon jelly

Ingredients for 6 people:
1lt of water, 250g of sugar, 90g of corn starch, 20g of cinnamon in sticks, pistachios as required

Method:

Leave the sticks of cinnamon to steep for at least 8 hours in a litre of water. When the time is up, bring the water to the boil and leave the infusion to stand for a whole day, then remove the cinnamon sticks and pour the flavoured water into a saucepan, mixing in the sieved corn starch. Add the sugar to the mixture, place the saucepan on a medium heat and stir.

When the mixture reaches boiling point ad becomes viscous, remove from the heat and leave to cool in ice-cream cups.

When it has cooled, place in the fridge until it takes on the consistency of a blancmange and then serve decorated with some pistachio grains.

Lemon jelly

Ingredients for 6 people:
800ml of water, 250g of sugar, 200ml of lemon juice, 90g of corn starch

Method:

Filter the lemon juice and pour it gradually into a saucepan containing water, mixing in the sieved corn starch.

Add the sugar to the mixture, place the saucepan on a medium heat and stir.

When it comes to the boil and takes on a viscous consistency, remove from the heat and place in ice-cream cups to cool.

When it has cooled, place in the fridge until it takes on the consistency of a blancmange and then serve cold.

Water melon jelly

Ingredients for 4 people: 1lt of water melon juice, 100-200g of sugar (depending on the natural sweetness of the juice), 90g of corn starch, powdered cinnamon and finely chopped pistachios as required, chocolate drops (optional), cubes of candied pumpkin (optional)

Method:

Cut a water melon into pieces and then puree it until you get a litre of juice. Filter the juice to remove the seeds and pour it gradually into a saucepan containing water, mixing in the sieved corn starch until you get a creamy mixture.

Add the sugar to the mixture, place the saucepan on a medium heat and stir carefully until it thickens and darkens (10-15 minutes).

Remove from the heat and leave to cool in another container. When it has cooled enough, add the candied pumpkin and chocolate drops and place in ice-cream cups. Place in the fridge until it takes on the consistency of a blancmange and, finally, decorate with a sprinkling of cinnamon, a few more chocolate drops and pistachio grains before serving.

Giuseppe Orlando, *www.dolcisiciliani.net*

"Biancomangiare"

Preparation about 60 minutes	*Ingredients for 4 people:*
	✓ 1l of almond milk
Difficulty average	✓ 100g of sugar
Recommended wine Baccadoro (Grillo), Az. Agr. Fondo Antico	✓ 200g of starch for cakes
	✓ a pinch of cinnamon

Method:

Get the milk directly from the fresh almonds. To do this, crush the shelled almonds in a mortar until you obtain a cream.

Pour the cream onto a napkin, tie it up like a sack and dip it several times into a cup of cold water, then squeeze the almond juice into a saucepan.

Alternatively, you can buy ready-made almond milk. Dissolve the starch in the almond milk, add the sugar and cinnamon, and heat on a very low flame, continually stirring, until the cream thickens. Place on a plate and serve cold.

Evelin Costa, *agavepalermo*

ladri di ricette

" *La cuccìa* "

Preparation about 960 minutes	*Ingredients for 4 people:*
Difficulty average	✓ 600g of wholegrain wheat
Recommended wine Al Hamen, Feudo Ramadin	✓ 400g of sugar
	✓ 800g of ricotta
	✓ 100g of chocolate drops
	✓ 2 spoonfuls of vanilla essence
	✓ powdered cinnamon as required

Method:

Soak the wheat for 3 days, changing the water every day. Cook on a low heat with water and salt for 6/8 hours until the wheat softens (you can also use a pressure cooker for 40 minutes). Drain and leave to cool. In the meantime, prepare the ricotta cream whisking it with the sugar and vanilla essence until you get a smooth mixture.

Leave to stand for 30 minutes. Mix the ricotta cream with the cooked wheat. Finally, add the chocolate and a dusting of cinnamon. Leave to stand for a few hours and serve. In some recipes candied fruit or orange peel are added.

History of "la cuccìa":

This delicious cake is traditionally made for Saint Lucy's Day on 13th December (especially in Siracusa and Palermo) and in the run up to Christmas. According to the legend, in Palermo, during a terrible famine, the population was dying of hunger when a ship unexpectedly arrived in the port carrying wheat. It was immediately distributed and, rather than wasting time milling it, people cooked it as it was. This happened on 13th December and, ever since, in celebration of Saint Lucy, believed to be responsible for the miracle, instead of eating bread or pasta, on this day people eat "la cuccìa", from the verb "cucciare" derived from "cocciu" ("chicco" or grain, from the Greek "kokkia"). Grains of wheat have a similar shape to eye pupils, recalling Saint Lucy who was blinded.

"Pignolata messinese"

Ingredients for the pastry:
350g of superfine flour, 6 egg yolks, 50 ml of pure alcohol for cakes, peanut oil
Ingredients for the chocolate icing:
150g of icing sugar, 150g of bitter cacao, 10ml of water, 75g of butter, a pinch of vanilla
Ingredients for the lemon icing:
200g of icing sugar, 2 egg whites, juice of 2 lemons

Method:

Beat the egg yolks and the alcohol in a bowl, then add the flour little by little, continuing to beat until you get a smooth mixture. Lay out the dough on a worktop making thin sticks. Cut into small pieces, each one 2cm long, or roll into balls. Fry the pieces a few at a time in hot peanut oil, turning them so that become golden brown, then place them on kitchen paper to absorb the excess oil. To make the chocolate icing, melt the butter in a pan on a low heat, adding the icing sugar, vanilla, sieved cacao and water a little at a time. The water must be added gradually until the mixture gains the right thickness. Leave to cool.

To make the lemon icing, pour the sugar into a saucepan and place on a low heat until it begins to filare, then put into a bowl adding the whisked egg whites a little at a time. Stir for a good while with a spoon, adding the lemon juice, until you get a soft white icing.

At this point place the pieces of fried "pignolata" pastry on a serving dish, making a rectangular pile, and cover one half with the chocolate icing and the other half with the lemon icing. Wait until the icing dries out before serving.

"Pignoccata alla palermitana"

Preparation	Ingredients for 4 people:
about 60 minutes	✓ 500g of cake flour
Difficulty easy	✓ 5 eggs
Recommended wine	✓ 100g of honey
Marsala Rossa,	✓ 200g of sugar
Carlo Pellegrino	✓ grated orange rind

Method:

Knead the flour with the eggs and half of the sugar. Split the dough into portions and smooth it with your hands until you get tubular strips about 1cm in diameter.

Then cut these into pieces of about 1cm and fry them in hot oil. When all the pastry is fried, pour the honey and the rest of the sugar into a saucepan with half a glass of water and heat until they dissolve. Remove from the heat and stir the fried pieces of pastry in the pan so that the honey sticks to them. Use a spoon to make small piles of "pignoccata", which then are left to cool on a marble top greased with a little oil.

"Cannoli"

Preparation about 120 minutes	*Ingredients for 4 people:* ✓ 400g of flour ✓ 1 egg ✓ salt ✓ 40g of sugar ✓ 40g of lard ✓ 90ml of Marsala	✓ seed oil *For the filling:* ✓ 500g of goat milk ricotta ✓ 5 tablespoons of icing sugar ✓ 2 fistfuls of chocolate drops ✓ pistachio grains as required
Difficulty easy		
Recommended wine Ben Ryè (Passito di Pantelleria), Donnafugata		

Method:

Mix the flour with the egg, salt, sugar, melted lard and Marsala. Knead well then roll out the pastry , not too thinly. Cut out discs of pastry and roll them around the special cylinders, sealing the edges well with water.

Fry the "cannoli" in not too hot oil. For the filling, add icing sugar and chocolate drops to the sieved ricotta. Fill the "cannoli" and roll them in the pistachio grains.

Pasticceria "Duomo", *Cefalù*

History of the "cannolo":

During the Roman period there was already a "canneolus farinario", "cannolo" flour. The Sicilian "cannolo", according to numerous sources, originated in Caltanissetta (in Arabic "Kalt el Nisdsa" - castle of women) home to the Emir's harem in the 12th century. It was once again the Arabs who invented this recipe using ricotta with sugar, candied fruit and pieces of chocolate. It is said that when the Normans arrived some of the women in the harem converted to Christianity and entered convents. These nuns handed down many of the Arab recipes they knew, including "cannolo". The shape of the "cannolo" was changed under Christianity, abandoning its original phallic form. We suggest that visitors to Sicily try the delicious traditional "cannoli" in Piana degli Albanesi. The expert local pastry chefs in Piana use the milk from sheep that graze on the plateau at an altitude of 3,000 feet. A truly 5 star "cannolo".

Sicilian Cassata

	Ingredients for 4 people:	✓ 250g of sugar
Preparation about 120 minutes	✓ 250g of almond flour	✓ 300g of flour
Difficulty difficult	✓ 250g of icing sugar	*For the filling:*
Recommended wine	✓ 1 tablespoon of glucose (or honey)	✓ 1kg of sheep milk ricotta
Marsala LP,	✓ water as required	✓ 400g of sugar
Pietro Pipitone Spanò	✓ food colouring	✓ chocolate drops
	For the sponge:	✓ candied fruit as required
	✓ 5 eggs	

Method:

Mix the almond flour with the icing sugar and glucose, adding a little water to make it easier to knead. Also add a little green food colouring dissolved in water and knead well. Leave to stand at room temperature for 15-20 minutes. To prepare the sponge, beat the eggs with the sugar, then add the flour, mixing carefully and then place in a baking tin. Bake in the oven at 180° for about 20 minutes. Roll out the marzipan pastry on a worktop sprinkled with icing sugar, making a layer about 1cm thick, then cut it into squares. Remove the crust from the sponge and cut some squares of the same size as the marzipan. Sprinkle a cake tin with icing sugar and line the sides with alternate squares of marzipan and sponge, cutting off any excess pieces.

Line the bottom of the cake tin with sponge cut into strips. Strain the ricotta into a bowl with sugar, then separate into two parts, adding chocolate drops to one. Fill the cake shell with ricotta cream, making sure it is compact, and finish off with the cut offs of marzipan and sponge. Turn out the cassata onto a plate and leave to stand for about twenty minutes.

Complete by coating the cassata with the remaining ricotta and sugar mixture and return to the fridge. Decorate with candied fruit.

Ricotta "cassatelle" (Cassatedde)

	For the puff pastry:	For the ricotta cream:
Preparation about 75 minutes	✓ 500g of reground flour	✓ 500g of sheep milk ricotta (already drained)
Difficulty average	✓ extra virgin olive oil	✓ 150g of sugar
Recommended wine Cigna La Miccia (Marsala Oro 5 Anni), Az. Agr. Marco De Bartoli	✓ 1 tablespoon of sugar	✓ 50g of dark chocolate in small flakes
	✓ 1 egg yolk	*For the decoration:*
	✓ a glass of dry Marsala	✓ icing sugar
	✓ 1 lemon rind	
	✓ 1 sachet of vanillin	
	✓ a large pinch of salt	

Method for the pastry:

Knead the ingredients: flour, sugar, oil, egg yolk, salt, lemon rind and add the dry Marsala little by little, until you get a dense mixture. Cover with a cloth and leave to stand for 30 minutes.

Method for the ricotta cream:

Sieve the ricotta with the sugar, add the dark chocolate. Roll out the pastry thinly and cut out discs, place a pile of ricotta cream on top and fold over the pastry to make a crescent moon shape. Fry in plenty of sunflower seed oil. Sprinkle with icing sugar and serve.

The "Cassatedda" is one of the oldest and best known cakes from the province of Trapani; try it,

I guarantee you will be glad you did.

Maria Piacentino - Il Casolare nelle Saline, *Nubia*

"Buccellato"

Preparation about 180 minutes	Ingredients:	✓ 200g of raisins
Difficulty average	✓ 500g of flour	✓ 200g of candied pumpkin
Recommended wine Vecchio Samperi, Az. Agr. Marco De Bartoli	✓ 250g of butter	✓ 150g of finely chopped toasted almonds
	✓ 150g of sugar	✓ 5 cloves
	✓ 3 eggs and a yolk	✓ 1 pinch of cinnamon
	✓ 100g of walnut kernels	✓ 1 glass of Marsala
	✓ 300g of dried figs	✓ candied cherries and oranges
	✓ 60g of finely chopped pistachios	
	✓ 100g of dark chocolate	

Method:

Knead the flour, butter, half a glass of Marsala, eggs and a pinch of salt until you obtain a smooth mixture. Wrap in a napkin and place in the fridge for 30 minutes. Prepare the filling by placing in a saucepan the finely chopped dried figs, the finely chopped roasted almonds, raisins, candied pumpkin, grated lemon, the dark chocolate, cloves, half a glass of Marsala and a pinch of cinnamon. Mix well and cook on a low heat for 20 minutes. Stretch out the dough in a rectangle to a thickness of about 1 cm.

Lay the cold filling mixture along the centre and close the dough making a roll. Then join the two ends, forming a doughnut shape. Use a fork to make some holes in the surface of the doughnut and then place in a greased baking tin. Cook in the oven at 180° for 40 minutes. Remove the "buccellato" from the oven and brush it with the beaten egg yolk, sprinkle on the pistachios and return to the oven for 10 more minutes. When cooked, decorate with the candied fruit. Leave to cool.

Rice doughnuts

	Ingredients for 6 people:	✓ salt
Preparation about 120 minutes	✓ 300g of rice	
Difficulty average	✓ 10g of brewer's yeast	
Recommended wine Malvasia delle Lipari, Hauner	✓ milk	
	✓ icing sugar	
	✓ powdered cinnamon	
	✓ peanut oil	

Method:

Place the rice in a saucepan with 5dl of milk, a similar amount of water and a pinch of salt. Heat the saucepan and bring to the boil; then move it to the oven on a medium heat and remove it when all the liquid has dried up. Tip the rice into a large bowl, add the yeast dissolved in a tablespoon of milk, mix well and after covering the bowl, leave it to stand at room temperature for at least an hour. Pour plenty of oil into a large frying pan, heat it well and then place the rice in the pan in small portions using a tablespoon.

Cook until golden brown, then place on kitchen paper to drain. Serve after sprinkling with a mixture of icing sugar and powdered cinnamon.

palermomania

"Sfince di San Giuseppe"

Preparation	Ingredients for 4 people:	
about 90 minutes	✓ 300g of flour for cakes	✓ 200g of sugar
Difficulty average	✓ 6 eggs and 6 egg yolks	✓ 100g of dark chocolate
Recommended wine	✓ 100g of butter	✓ 50g of candied pumpkin
Zibbibo liquoroso,	✓ a pinch of salt	✓ candied orange peel
Cantine Grasso	✓ 425g of water	
	✓ 300g of fresh ricotta	

Method:

Heat a saucepan containing water and butter. When the water boils and the butter has melted, remove from the heat and pour the flour into the saucepan, adding a pinch of salt. Stir quickly and mix the ingredients together. Return to the heat until the flour has all been removed from the sides of the pan (about 10 minutes).

Leave to cool and mix again adding the egg yolks, one by one, and then the whites in the same way, after whisking them, waiting until they have been well absorbed each time before passing on to the next yolk or white. The mixture should be soft and smooth. Place it in a pan of boiling oil using a spoon and fry. For each "sfincia", you need 2 or 3 spoonfuls of mixture. Let them turn golden brown on both sides and place on kitchen paper to dry. Leave to cool and then pour the ricotta cream on each one. To make the cream, mix together the sugar, chocolate and candied pumpkin. Finally, decorate with candied orange peel.

Almond pastries

Preparation about 75 minutes	*Ingredients for 6 people:*
Difficulty average	✓ 500g of shelled almonds
Recommended wine Vecchio Florio vino Marsala Superiore, Florio	✓ 500g of sugar
	✓ 4 egg whites
	✓ flour
	✓ icing sugar
	✓ lemon, vanilla, candied cherries

Method:

Peel and finely chop the almonds, add some grated lemon rind and a little vanilla. Whip up the egg whites and add them to the mixture, add the sugar and mix. If the dough is too soft, add a few spoonfuls of flour. Grease a baking tin and use a baking syringe to place clumps of dough at regular intervals. Decorate the pastries with candied cherries and bake in the oven at a very low temperature, until they are a light golden colour.

Remove from the oven, leave to cool, sprinkle with icing sugar and serve.

"Martorana" fruit

Preparation	Ingredients for 4 people:
about 90 minutes	✓ 2kg of sugar
Difficulty difficult	✓ 500g of almonds
Recommended wine	✓ 400g of glucose
Vino alla Mandorla,	✓ flour
Turrisi di Castelmola	

Method:

After obtaining a compact and smooth mixture you can make cakes in the shape of fruit. Press the mixture into the special chalk moulds, removing any excess: apples, pears, chestnuts, etc. Before painting the fruits with vegetable colours leave them to dry well (1 or 2 days). Polish them with special products for food. Place on a plate and decorate with strips of coloured paper.

Marzipan, "martorana" fruit, "pasta reale" (almond paste):

Since almonds are widely grown in Sicily, it is possible that sweet dishes made from ground almonds were around as early as the Greek colonisation.

Almond paste is also known as marzipan, a term that refers to the container used for keeping the bread made from almonds and sugar, deriving from the Arabic word "manthaban". According to tradition, during the Norman period, the Benedictine nuns from the convent founded in 1194 by the noblewoman Eloisa Martorana, and linked to the Palermo church of Santa Maria dell'Ammiraglio, first made cakes from almond paste in the shape of fruit (probably citrus fruits) in 1308. They then hung them from the trees in the convent garden to replace the harvested fruit as decoration when Pope Clement visited. These lovely creations easily fool those who see them for the first time. This is why, first in Palermo and then all over Sicily, they were called "Martorana" fruit, from the name of the convent.

The name "pasta reale" originated in 1799, when King Ferdinand III (King of the Two Sicilies) visited Palermo and was offered delicious cakes, fit for a King ("Re" in Italian). Thus, the name "Pasta Reale".

Almond nougat
"Minnulata or Cubbaita"

Preparation about 60 minutes	*Ingredients for 4 people:*
Difficulty average	✓ 300g of dried almonds
Recommended wine Grillo, Alessandro di Camporeale	✓ 300g of sugar
	✓ 50g of honey

Method:

Toast the almonds (without the skin) on a low heat in a non-stick pan, until they are golden brown. Add the sugar to the frying pan, mixing continually.

When the sugar has melted, add the honey while stirring and pour everything onto a marble top greased with oil. Flatten the mixture until it is about 5mm thick. Cut it with a kitchen knife while it is still warm. Leave it to cool before eating.

Curiosity:

"Torronari" (nougat sellers) and stalls selling "calia" (toasted and salted chick peas) and "simenza" (toasted and salted pumpkin seeds) are always to be found at traditional Sicilian festivals and fairs. Nougat is of Arab origin. The Sicilian name for it, "cubbaita" (as it is still called in Caltanissetta), derives from the Arabic "qubbayt". There are numerous versions all over Sicily: with hazelnuts and peanuts, with toasted chick peas cooked in honey, soft and white with almonds and dried fruit, with chocolate and with almonds and pistachios. Originally, however, it was made simply with almonds, honey and "giuggiulena" (sesame seeds).

Orange peel in chocolate

Recommended wine
Marsala GD, Mirabella

Ingredients for 6 people:
✓ 10g of butter
✓ 220g of dark chocolate
✓ candied orange peel

Method:

In order to get the best results the oranges used should not be too ripe. Wash the fruit well in running water. Pierce the skin using pins. Soak in water for 48 hours to remove the sourness and distend the fibres. Then, cut the oranges into segments, remove the pulp with a knife and cut the peel into strips about 0.5cm wide. Place into cold water, bring to the boil and simmer for as long as needed; you can check if the peel is cooked by using a pin (if it penetrates the fruit easily you can move on to the next phase). Remove the water without touching the fruit with your hands. Dissolve 600g of sugar in 1l of water; bring to the boil (36 degrees Brix: Brix is the density of sugar dissolved in a liquid. Thus, 1 degree Brix corresponds to one part solid sugar and 99 parts liquid), pour onto the parboiled fruit placed on a grille. Cover with cling film and leave to steep for 24 hours at room temperature. Repeat this procedure for a week, increasing the syrup by 5-7 degrees Brix each day, until you reach 70 degrees Brix. Once you have obtained your candied orange peel strips, dry them on kitchen paper. Melt the dark chocolate (70% cacao) in the microwave, being careful not to exceed 50°C. Finally, glaze the orange peel with the chocolate.

Pasticceria "Scimeca", *Caccamo*

Quince jelly

Preparation	Ingredients for 6 people:
about 60 minutes	✓ 1kg of quinces
Difficulty average	✓ 1kg of sugar
Recommended wine	✓ 2 lemons
Grappa barricata	
Harmonium, Firriato	

Method:

Peel the quinces and cut them into segments. Cook in boiling water. Drain, dampen them with cold water and pass through a sieve.

Weigh and add 1kg of sugar and the juice of 2 lemons for every 800g of pulp. Place everything in a saucepan on the heat and cook for about 10 minutes, stirring continually. Heat the special terracotta moulds in the oven and pour in the mixture. If you haven't got the moulds you can use small bowls. Leave the jelly to dry in a cool ventilated place and, when a thin layer of sugar has formed, remove from the mould and leave to dry on the other side.

"Mostarda"

Preparation	Ingredients for 6 people:	✓ 1 clove
about 60 minutes	✓ 3lt of wine must	✓ nutmeg
Difficulty average	✓ 60g of vine ash	
Recommended wine	✓ 180g of starch for cakes	
Grappa Obli,	✓ 50g of toasted almonds	
Azienda Enza La Fauc	✓ a pinch of cinnamon	
	✓ 1/2 sachet of vanilla	

Method:

Place the must in a saucepan and cook with the vine ash until a third of it has evaporated. Leave to stand for 12 hours, then filter several times.

Measure the liquid and add 90g of starch for every litre of must, stir, making sure that no lumps form, filtering again if necessary. Return to a low heat and, when the mixture begins to thicken, add the cinnamon, clove, a little grated nutmeg and the finely chopped almonds. Stir for a few more minutes, then test how well it is cooked by dropping a little of the mixture onto a slanted plate: if it doesn't slide down the plate, then it is ready. Place in the appropriate dampened terracotta moulds and leave to dry in a well aired environment.

Prickly pear jam

Ingredients: 1kg of prickly pear pulp, a glass of water, the juice and rind of a lemon, 500g of sugar

Method:

After peeling the prickly pears, cut their pulp into very small cubes and tip them into a saucepan. Heat the saucepan, add the glass of water to the prickly pear pulp. Bring to the boil until the cubes of prickly pear become mushy, then remove the saucepan from the heat and pass the pulp through a sieve to remove the seeds. Return the pulp to the saucepan and heat again; in the meantime, grate the rind of a lemon and squeeze the juice.

Add the sugar to the pulp and when it begins to boil again, add the lemon juice and the grated rind. Boil for about 40 minutes longer and then, when the mixture has thickened, turn off the heat and transfer the prickly pear jam into sterilised glass jars.

Close the jars well and turn them upside down so as to create the vacuum that will help preserve the prickly pear jam for a long time.

Index

Printed in May 2016
by Avvenire 2000 via Area Artigianale, agglomerato ASI
98129 Larderia Inferiore - Messina